# SPROUTING WISDOM: HERB GARDENING MADE SIMPLE

HOW TO GROW, HARVEST, PRESERVE, & COOK WITH HERBS

MACKENZIE GAYLE

# CONTENTS

# INTRODUCTION

---

*In the magic of herbs, we find harmony with nature.*

— UNKNOWN

---

Are you trying to grow your own herb garden, but you're not sure where to start? Have you tried growing a few herbs but ended up with droopy, wilted plants that were a far cry from the herb plants you had envisioned? Did these dangly plantlings dash your dreams of cooking with healthy, organic herbs from your own garden?

If you've answered yes to any of these questions, then we already have something in common! Taking a look at my current herb garden, often referred to as my *pride and joy*, you'd never believe that it started out as a few pots of parsley and oregano on the kitchen windowsill. Looking at my healthy herblings (as I like to call them), you'd never know that their predecessors endured all sorts of newbie mistakes. Indeed, they encountered everything from over-watering to drowning, with some incorrect harvesting thrown in for good measure!

In those early days, the many things that can—and often do—go wrong led me to believe that I didn't have a semblance of a green thumb. However, I was determined to see it through and not give up until I could successfully grow a single herb. As a stubborn person, I wasn't about to let a bunch of teeny herblings break my spirit!

Imagine my delight at being able to grow a tiny little parsley herbling in my kitchen windowsill until it was big enough to be transferred to a larger pot on the patio, just outside the kitchen door. Despite having eventually managed to successfully grow a much larger herb garden in my backyard, my precious parsley pot still stands in its place on the patio—a tall and happy reminder that growing an herb garden from scratch, with only the most basic resources, isn't impossible.

That's where many novice gardeners give up—thinking that growing an herb garden is impossible. Researching the ins and outs of herb gardening can be overwhelming. This is because many articles, books, and supposed guides simply overcomplicate the whole process. It's easy to see why many newbies lose interest!

That's where I come in. After reading many of these over complicated how-to manuals, I decided to create a guide that streamlined the whole process. By focusing on my own experience from beginner to proficiency, I have been able to create a simple guide that makes it easy to start and successfully grow your own herb garden, no matter your experience level or available space.

By reading my hands-on guide, you'll be able to start your own herb garden with the space and experience you have. I'll also simplify aspects such as finding the right spot, understanding your herbs' basic needs, pest control, and growing herbs from cuttings. I'll also be addressing the most common herb gardening issues and how to over-come them.

Furthermore, I'll share a few tips to help you use your freshly grown herbs in your recipes and how best to benefit from their medicinal properties. We'll also go over the easiest herbs that you should start growing. The trick is to start with the strong, easy-to-grow variants that don't need much pampering to grow. Choosing the herbs that are easiest to grow is a huge confidence boost! It will only be a matter of time before you share my satisfaction of not having to shop for herbs. Believe me when I tell you that homegrown herbs add a delicious flavor to every dish!

My goal is to provide you with all the information and tips you'll need as you embark on your herb gardening journey. Once you see how easy it really is, you'll be excited to get started!

With that said, let's dive into Chapter 1, where I share the easiest ways to recognize the appearance of the most common herbs, as well as the first steps to crafting the ideal growth environment. Let's take that first step on your journey to creating a functional herb garden!

# 1

# GETTING TO KNOW YOUR HERBS INSIDE OUT

*I grow my own vegetables and herbs. I like being able to tell people that the lunch I'm serving started out as a seed in my yard.*

— CURTIS STONE

I f you've ever given the Consumer Price Index Report from the U.S. Department of Labor even just a passing glance, you'd have read that the average American is spending an estimated $253 more a month on groceries and other necessities (Cariaga, 2023).

Choosing to grow your own herbs as a means to reduce the amount of money you spend on groceries may be a common motivator. Alternatively, your reason for wanting an herb garden could be an attempt to reduce your and your family's exposure to preservatives, fillers, and potential exposure to toxic chemicals.

That said, if you're still on the fence about whether an herb garden is something you really want to have, keep reading, as I'm going to highlight a few good reasons why everyone should be growing even the smallest herb garden.

WHY CREATE AN HERB GARDEN?

You may have already made up your mind to start gardening. But, why start with herbs? Here are a few good reasons to consider:

1. **Easy to grow:** Overall, herbs are hands down the easiest edibles to grow. They are determined to grow, and for the most part, they can grow just about anywhere. If you've never grown a plant in

your life, starting with herbs is the way to go. Furthermore, since many herbs can be grown from cuttings or root division, you won't have to spend much money getting your hands on a few herblings. (Chapter 3 takes a look at the top five herbs to start with)

2. **Thrive in containers:** Unlike some veggies and certain flower types that require a large area for their root systems, herbs not only grow but thrive in containers. This means you can plant a few herblings in some small pots on your windowsill, and with a bit of TLC, they'll be growing in no time. (More about container growing in the next chapter)

3. **Excellent for eating:** If you love cooking with herbs as much as I do, then this will most likely be your number one reason. If, however, you've recently decided to improve your eating habits or add more organic options to your meal plans, then the right types of herbs are the best place to start. Once you start adding fresh herbs to your dishes, you'll never buy dried store-bought versions again! (More about cooking with herbs in Chapter 7)

4. **Add fragrance to your living space:** Many herbs such as lavender, scented geraniums, basil, thyme, and rosemary are just a few of the herbs that offer amazing fragrances to the areas they're planted in. Pick your favorite herb and plant it in a few

pots around your home to have natural air fresheners.

5. **Create a wonderful garden:** Herbs such as lavender, rosemary, and hedge germander can be grown and shaped to make stunning low hedges around an existing or boring garden. The purple flowers from lavender, the yellow from dill, the red hues from red clover, and the white or pink flowers from rosemary shrubs all make beautiful additions to any new or existing garden.

6. **Powerful medicinal properties:** Many herbs have medicinal properties that make them a firm favorite in my garden. For instance, oregano has excellent antioxidant levels, while rosemary works well to aid digestion. (More about medicinal herbs in Chapter 8)

## UNDERSTANDING HERB LINGO

I've found that many newbies easily get frustrated with the terms and phrases used in some manuals and how-to guides. If you're completely new to gardening, being met with a rush of gardening terms when you're standing in front of a Mr. Know-It-All at the garden center can add to the frustration. Right?

Fortunately, I know how you feel. As such, I've decided to include a short list highlighting the lingo often used in the herb gardening process. Being familiar with these terms will make it easier for you to speak to local garden center agents when you're looking for something specific.

- **Annuals:** Annual plants and herbs are those that complete their whole life cycle within a single growing season. In these instances, a dormant seed is the only part of the plant that survives, which means that the plant needs to be regrown for the next season. Examples of annual herbs include basil, cilantro (often also called coriander), dill, chamomile, marjoram, fennel, and chervil.

- **Perennials:** Perennials, on the other hand, can survive for many years or growing seasons. They won't need to be replanted after the end of the season, as they will grow back from the roots. Typical examples of perennials are mint, thyme, oregano, rosemary, sage, tarragon, lavender, garlic chives, and lemon balm.

- **Compost:** The term compost typically refers to decayed organic material that is used as fertilizer for growing plants and herbs. Compost can be made from browns (dry leaves, plant stalks, and twigs), greens (grass clippings), and organic materials (vegetable peels and food scraps). You can buy compost or make your own.

- **Mulch:** Mulch is any material that can be laid or spread over the soil surface. Essentially, it's used for a covering and keeps moisture in the soil. It also extends the time between waterings.

Common mulch options to consider for your herb plants are cedar, hardwood, or cypress wood chips.

- **Pruning:** Herbs, like trees and shrubs, require pruning, which involves cutting away any dead or damaged stems, leaves, and branches. Doing this not only deters disease on the plant but also encourages growth.

- **Harvest:** Harvesting your herbs refers to the process of snipping your plants when there is enough foliage to use as well as supporting new growth. It's a good idea to harvest no more than one-third of the plant so that it can continue producing more foliage.

- **Culinary herbs:** Culinary herbs are those that are used to add flavor and fragrance to food. They can be added to salads, stews, sauces, casseroles, and meat and poultry marinades and dishes. Top culinary herbs include thyme, rosemary, dill, sage, mint, basil, and cilantro.

- **Medicinal herbs:** As the name indicates, medicinal herbs are those used in traditional medicinal practices. These are typically used to treat inflammation and boost the immune system. The most common examples are rosemary, garlic, lavender, valerian, turmeric, and basil.

- **Organic gardening:** Opting for organic gardening means that you reject all artificial agricultural practices such as pesticides. Organic gardening means you're only using other plants, animals, and mineral fuels to nourish and sustain your herb plants. Common examples of this include using animal manure rather than chemical fertilizers.

- **Heirloom plants:** Heirloom plants are lines of plants that have been passed around families or gardening groups. To create an heirloom plant, you'll use cuttings or sections of the original plant to grow other plants for fellow gardeners.
- **Hardiness zones:** Hardiness zones measure an herb's ability to withstand cold winter temperatures. Typically, this is measured using a hardiness rating system that highlights the minimum temperature they can withstand. You'll need to be aware of this as you transplant herblings in your backyard.
- **Compassion planting:** Compassion planting refers to the mindful practice of setting an intention before and during your herb planting process. Ever heard your grandmother say that you need to plant your flowers with a good heart? Well, that's what it means!
- **Aerating:** Aerating generally involves perforating the soil by adding small holes to enable water, air, and nutrients to penetrate the roots. Typically, this creates a stronger and more vigorous foundation for your herb roots.
- **pH level:** The pH level is the value used to measure the acidity of the soil and water. This is

necessary as some herbs require a more acidic soil environment than others. The majority of herbs require well-drained soil with a pH that ranges between 6.0 and 7.5. Simple pH strips can be used to test the soil and water pH levels.

- **Propagation:** Generally, propagation is the process of growing multiple plants from a single plant. This is usually done by taking a cutting from the "mother plant" and nursing it until it grows its own roots. The most common herbs that you can propagate include thyme, sage, oregano, basil, mint, lavender, and rosemary.

## A CLOSER LOOK AT YOUR HERB COMPANIONS

Have you ever noticed that the gardens (herbs, flowers, and even veggies) you admire the most are usually made up of several little groups of plants growing together? There's a good reason for this.

Companion planting has been around since, well, forever. It refers to the concept that certain plants should be grown together so that they can physically support each other. A companion plant can either provide shade or a stem for a creeping plant to lean against. Furthermore, companion plants can also use their fragrance to keep pests away from the primary herb.

If you're planning to set up an outdoor garden, I would recommend adding a few companion plants to help you give your little herblings the best chance of survival. Keep in mind that just as certain plants are good for your herbs, others may not be so great. To make the process much easier, I've compiled a list of the most common herbs with their best companions as well as a few options to avoid.

| Herb | Suitable companion plants | Avoid planting near herb |
|---|---|---|
| Parsley | Asparagus, tomato | None |
| Basil | Parsley, tomatoes | None |
| Dill | Potatoes, rosemary, onions, peppermint, tomatoes | Carrots |
| Chives | Carrots, tomatoes | Beans, peas |
| Rosemary | Beans, cabbage, garlic | Mildew-prone plants such as pumpkins |
| Thyme | Strawberries | Basil, chives, tarragon |
| Oregano | Squash, beans, eggplant | Raspberries, mint |
| Sage | Rosemary, lettuce | Rue |
| Chamomile | Onions, cucumbers | Fennel, dill |
| Lavender | Fruit trees, echinacea, rosemary, oregano | Perennials or annuals that require a lot of water |
| Cilantro | Dill, spinach | None |

There can be a number of reasons as to why some plants don't make good companions. However, the most prominent has to do with the water requirements of different plants. For instance, planting an herb next to a plant that requires excessive water may cause root rot in the herb. In other cases, some herbs (such as chamomile) require less sunlight and wouldn't do well when planted next to sun lovers such as dill and fennel.

It's worth noting that, despite its aromatic fragrance, it's often not a good idea to plant any of the mint or peppermint variants directly in your garden. With their sprawling nature, they can quickly overtake your garden. This can be harmful to herbs such as oregano. To grow mint, keeping it in a container will make it easier to manage.

Tomatoes are another plant that's easy to grow and makes a wonderful companion to many herbs. Not only do they deter a wide range of pests, but they also reduce the onset of plant disease as well as enhance pollination. It's for this reason that I grow tomatoes side by side with most of my herbs. A plus here is that they're as wonderful to cook with as my delicious herbs!

### Crafting the Ideal Growth Environment

When you start listing the considerations to keep in mind as you embark on your herb gardening journey, it's important to start with an understanding of the ideal growth environment. Knowing what your herblings need in order to grow successfully will help you narrow down the best place to create the garden.

So, if you have a large backyard spot in mind, but the area never gets any sun or has high levels of clay soil, all that devoted space will be for naught. Keep in mind that some herbs have very specific requirements, but, for the most part, the average herbs all have the same requirements. Let's take a look at the most prominent growth environment you'll need to cultivate.

*Light*

As with most plants, the most important factor to consider when narrowing down your herb garden location is the amount of sunlight required. Here's how your different options stack up:

- **Outdoors:** Most herbs require at least six hours of direct sunlight. If you can place them in an area where they can get all day sun, this would be an even better option.
- **Indoors:** As with outdoor herbs, indoor plants need at least six hours of direct sunlight. This is why herbs do well in windowsills that have a southern exposure. If you feel that your herbs aren't getting enough sun in their indoor location, you can always place them 6 to 12 inches from two 40-watt, cool white fluorescent bulbs for about 14 hours. Herbs that aren't exposed to the right amount of light will have smaller leaves, a reduced aroma, and will be thin and spindly. If you're going to grow your herbs on a windowsill, I recommend rotating the pots often to ensure that each side of the plant gets adequate light to ensure uniform growth.

- **Vertical:** For vertical gardening, your herbs will require as much natural light as those in windowsills. Wherever possible, set up your vertical garden in an area that faces south. If your vertical garden doesn't get as much sun as necessary, it's a good idea to take a tip from agricultural scientists. They suggest using red, blue, and white lights that shine on your herbs as these are the three colors that promote plant growth where sunlight is limited (Modular Farming, 2021).

## Soil Type

Fortunately, most herbs will be quite content with typical garden soil, provided they have good drainage. When you're buying soil for the first time, either to plant herbs in containers or pots for your windowsill, you may want to start with loamier soil. You can also use high-quality potting soil but be sure to add a little sand to create the perfect herbling environment. Alternatively, you can opt for a potting soil mix such as PRO-MIX, which is lighter and fluffier and ideal for most herbs.

## Drainage

All pots and containers used for herb gardening should have good drainage holes in the bottom. It's as simple as using a drill to make several holes every 3 to 4 inches. One of the easiest ways to kill your precious little herblings is to overwater in a pot or container with poor drainage. I'll cover soil and drainage in a little more detail in Chapter 4.

### From Garden to Kitchen: A Culinary Journey

As I've already mentioned, adding herbs to your favorite dishes can significantly elevate the flavor profile of just about any dish.

It's also true that certain herbs are better for meat-based dishes while others are typically used to flavor salads and vegetarian dishes. I'll highlight the benefits of cooking with fresh herbs in Chapter 7, so keep reading for that!

Some herbs also have amazing anti-inflammatory properties that not only aid digestion but also boost memory. Chapter 8 takes an extensive look at the health benefits of some of the more commonly grown herbs.

Fortunately, herbs are super easy to preserve which extends their shelf-life, ensuring you have a constant supply for your kitchen and medicinal needs. Read all about techniques such as drying, freezing, and even making herb-infused oils in Chapter 6.

Now that you know what's coming in the next few chapters, you should be getting more excited about starting on your incredible herb gardening journey! In fact, it's time to take a look at the best options to create your green canvas. What will suit your situation better—backyard, windowsills, or containers? Read on to find out!

# 2

# CHOOSING YOUR GREEN CANVAS: BACKYARD, CONTAINER, OR WINDOW BOX

*I like muddling things up; and if an herb looks nice in a border, then why not grow it there? Why not grow anything anywhere so long as it looks right where it is? That is, surely, the art of gardening.*

— VITA SACKVILLE-WEST

The most appealing aspect of starting an herb garden is that you can grow it just about anywhere. So, this is the point where you ignore all those overly complex manuals that suggest you need a large space of land to even get started. Whether you live in a suburban home with a large backyard, or a small, modern, city apartment, the reality is that you absolutely can have an herb garden.

In my years of helping novice gardeners get started, I've seen people have as much success in tiny areas as those who have large spaces. The secret lies in understanding your environment, the pros and cons of your various options, and then eventually making the most out of your chosen space. Essentially, there are three major types of spaces you can consider. These include the following:

- backyard herb gardening
- container herb gardening
- indoor herb gardening

Let's take a look at each option in a little more detail to help you identify which option seems most appealing to you.

## EMBRACING THE EXPANSE: BACKYARD HERB GARDENING

As the name implies, backyard gardening refers to growing your herbs in your outdoor space. Creating a garden in the backyard allows you to grow a diverse variety of herbs. It also enables you to grow a large number of your favorite herbs.

With backyard gardens, you can cordon off a section of the space and create the perfect herb habitat. Here you can plant your herbs directly in the ground (if the soil is right) or you can use standalone containers such as those used in raised bed gardens. These are excellent options for areas where the soil may not be nutritious enough to sustain your little herblings.

As with all types of gardening, there are a few pros and cons to consider before you dig up your backyard. Let's take a look at them.

**Pros**

- You can experiment with a wide range of different herbs.
- Successful herb gardens can become a source of income.
- Growing herbs that you enjoy cooking with reduces the need to buy store-bought herbs and you always have fresh herbs on hand.

- Organic herbs are healthier and make a wonderful addition to any recipe.
- A well-maintained herb garden can add curb appeal to your property.

**Cons**

- Regular weeding is required to keep invasive plants from destroying your garden.
- Soil moisture levels need to be monitored to ensure correct drainage.
- It can be time-consuming to tend to a larger space.

I'm not going to beat around the bush—a backyard herb garden is a lot of work, especially if you're growing a diverse range of herbs. However, I must also point out that the benefits far outweigh the drawbacks. Stepping out into my herb garden and being greeted by the subtle fragrance of thyme, the refreshing aroma of mint, and the warm, soft scent of rosemary is soothing to my soul. Not to mention, they make for a peaceful green space to relax in. And, of course, there's the wonderful addition to just about all of my recipes—it's simply magic!

## COMPACT AND CONVENIENT: CONTAINER HERB GARDENING

If your living space lacks the advantage of ample outdoor space, but you have a small courtyard, container gardening may be the solution you've been looking for!

Simply put, container gardening involves growing your herbs in pots and planters. Some creative gardeners even repurpose old household items such as teapots, baskets, boots, or old wheelbarrows and turn them into container gardens. The only real criterion is that your container be made of safe material that's strong enough to hold the required soil and allow for adequate drainage. Let's take a look at the pros and cons of container gardening.

**Pros**

- Just about any container can be repurposed into a mini garden.
- Since containers are smaller, it's easier to control the soil and water conditions—this is beneficial to herbs that require specific growing conditions.
- Containers can be moved to avoid exposure to severe weather conditions.
- You can take containers with you when you move, making this a great option for renters or people who are only living in a specific place temporarily.
- It's easy to decorate containers to create a unique garden space that matches your outdoor decor

style and gives a drab courtyard a complete makeover.

- You can choose the size of your containers based on your space and herb requirements.
- Containers can be used to create vertical gardens along walls or balconies.

**Cons**

- Smaller spaces may limit the number of containers you can keep, which in turn limits your quantity of herbs.
- Using smaller containers may cause soil to dry out faster, which will require more frequent watering.

## WINDOWSILL WONDER: GROWING HERBS INDOORS

More good news is that if your outdoor space is very limited or nonexistent, you still have another option to consider. A windowsill with sufficient sunlight can make the perfect spot for a few pots of herbs.

Keep in mind that if you're considering this option, south-facing windows are the ideal option. This is because they receive the ideal amount of sunlight which is one of the most critical factors for growing herbs. The pros and cons of opting for growing herbs on your windowsill are listed below.

**Pros**

- Any container that fits in the windowsill can be used to grow your herblings in—popular options include jars, painted coffee tins, and even streamlined hydroponic systems specifically designed for indoor herb gardening.
- If you're using the kitchen windowsill, then your herbs are close at hand for adding to cooking.
- Fragrant herbs can add a pleasant aroma to your home and in some instances even deter bugs such as spiders, ants, and cockroaches.
- Greenery in your home adds a splash of color to your interior decor.

**Cons**

- Windowsill gardens require special care to ensure that they aren't overwatered and also receive adequate sunlight.
- It may be necessary to supplement sunlight with grow lights during the winter months, especially if you live in a dark apartment.
- Indoor air is drier, which can result in herbs drying out—this may require occasionally misting the herbs to provide the humidity they need to grow.

## SPREAD OUT AND UPWARD: VERTICAL HERB GARDENING

If you really don't have available space, another option worth considering is vertical gardening. While many people add vertical gardening to their existing gardens as an aesthetic feature, the main reason gardeners often choose vertical gardening is due to space constraints.

As the name implies, vertical gardening involves designing your garden in a vertical direction. In these instances, gardeners will use trellises to hold pots of plants. These types of gardening options are very common in urban settings such as apartments where yard, courtyard, or balcony space is limited. All you need is an empty wall to secure your trellises (or anything you're using to secure pots to the wall) and, of course, adequate sunlight.

There are a few pros and cons to vertical gardening which you should review before choosing this option.

**Pros**

- They are ideal for areas where space is limited.
- Plants grown vertically are safe from plant-munching.
- There is less risk of overcrowding, as is often the case with pots placed too closely together on the ground. This, in turn, allows for better air

circulation which increases exposure to sunlight and minimizes the risk of fungal diseases.

- Herbs arranged in a vertical garden experience less soil erosion as exposure to wind and rain is likely less.
- Plants are less inclined to be damaged by severe wind, rain, or even snow as gardeners often secure the stems of taller plants to the trellises or stakes, they're using for the initial vertical structure.
- Since the plants are not on the ground, there's less bending and kneeling, which is great for individuals who find these functions difficult.

**Cons**

- Vertical gardening requires more maintenance than other methods. Limited space means you will have to prune and fertilize more often to compensate for the space constraints.
- If the plants are in an area where they don't receive regular sunlight or rainwater, they could become dry.

I want to point out that it's not uncommon for gardeners to combine vertical methods with their regular options. Adding a few trellises to your existing garden is an excellent way to separate your herbs from your flowers and shrubs. It really is as simple as securing a few pots to an empty wall. Keep in mind that they should receive adequate sunlight and you should be able to reach the highest pots without too much effort. Remember, you will have to fertilize, prune, and de-weed the higher plants as well.

One of the aspects that I really enjoy about vertical gardens is that they allow you to be creative with your herb garden. You can use pots of different shapes, colors, and sizes to really make your garden come alive!

## YOUR GARDEN, YOUR CHOICE: MAKING THE DECISION

Ultimately, where you place your herb garden boils down to factors such as space, amount of sunlight, and, of course, your personal preference. It's not uncommon for budding gardeners to start a tiny herb garden on their windowsills before moving it out into the great big yard.

When you're considering the location of your new herb garden, there are a few pointers to consider before finalizing your decision. These are listed below.

- **Your daily routine:** Before you set up your garden, it's important to assess how much time you can devote to it each day. Keep in mind that some herbs will need regular attention in the form of weeding the garden and watering. It's also worth noting that some herbs may require more attention than others. If you already have a busy schedule, it may be a good idea to start with a small windowsill garden in the kitchen. You can easily water this type of garden while you're cooking or doing dishes. Remember that your garden shouldn't feel like a chore, otherwise, you'll soon lose interest.

- **Available space:** Assess the different spaces you have. Be sure to check whether or not they receive the right amount of sunlight. We'll cover this in more detail in the next chapter. Also, ask yourself where you'd enjoy gardening the most. If you have a specific nook in the backyard where the sun is just right and you love sitting out there, gardening may seem like less of a chore and more like part of your relaxation routine.

- **Watering options:** It's also important to consider how you're going to be watering the herb garden. Windowsill gardens are easy enough to water with a bottle or watering can, however, containers in the side courtyard may be a bit of a distance from the nearest tap. Once again, walking up and down with a heavy watering can in your hand can start feeling like too much of a chore after some time. The closer your garden is to a water source, the easier and more convenient it will be for you to keep your herblings happy and healthy!

Whichever location you choose, always remember that the joy of herb gardening lies in nurturing your herblings, watching them grow into big, strong herbs, and finally using them in your culinary creations or medicines. If you enjoy cooking, then you'll feel immensely proud when you use your own grown herbs to season your family's meals. Knowing that you've nurtured these little herbs from seeds or seedlings to flourishing, nutritious plants is very rewarding!

Once you've decided on where you want to grow your first herb garden, it's time to look at the components needed to start your garden from scratch. The next chapter takes a look at the required sun, tools needed, and getting your seedlings in the ground. Stay tuned!

# 3

# SOWING THE SEEDS OF SUCCESS: YOUR STEP-BY-STEP GUIDE TO STARTING AN HERB GARDEN

*What is a paradise, but, a garden, an orchid of trees and herbs, full of pleasure and nothing there but delights.*

— WILLIAM LAWSON

Putting your thoughts of being the keeper of a wonderful herb garden into action is often the most difficult hurdle to overcome. Having a clearer idea of how to choose the best spot for your first garden is only the first step. The next step is choosing a handful of herbs to get you started.

My biggest tip in choosing herbs is always to opt for a few that you are going to use the most in your recipes. Popular choices are often parsley, chives, and even mint. If you don't have specific herbs in mind, I recommend starting with those listed in the next section.

## SELECTING YOUR STARTER HERBS: FOCUSING ON THE FABULOUS FIVE

Most potential gardeners dream of growing as many herbs as possible. However, I always recommend that first-time gardeners start with a few of the easiest-to-grow herbs that are easy to use in both recipes and medicine.

Typically, there are five top herbs, commonly referred to as the fabulous five, that experts recommend you start with. As the name implies, this selection is made up of the five most common herbs that are the simplest to grow as well as the most versatile in recipes all while also having a bunch of excellent medicinal purposes. I am happy to announce that all of these wonderful herbs have a prime spot in my garden, and I use them all the time!

Here's my list of the fabulous five herbs to get you started:

- **Parsley:** For most people, parsley is a must-have. This is mostly because it can be used as a garnish as well as a flavoring and is usually a staple in most traditional and modern pairings. Moreover, you can create parsley tea to treat urinary tract infections or simply blitz it into your favorite pesto sauce.

- **Rosemary:** Anyone who enjoys chicken noodle soup or roast potatoes will vouch for the wonderful taste that rosemary adds to these two dishes. The fact that rosemary is a perennial means it's just as easy to grow as it is to cook with. You can easily grow rosemary in most soil types and climates. Additionally, the oil in a rosemary herb can be extracted and used to drizzle over salads and various meat dishes for a delicious flavor boost!

- **Mint:** It has to be said—mint is the ultimate herb to give your gardening skills a much-needed boost. The main reason for this is that mint is an overzealous grower and will grow wherever you plant it, whether it's the backyard, your container collection in the courtyard, or even your kitchen windowsill. There is a catch with mint that I must share with you, though. Mint tends to overwhelm your whole garden if you're not careful. I would also recommend that you, as a first-time mint grower, opt for adding the herb to a pot or container so that you can manage it better. Mint is wonderful for creating a soothing tea, adding to your smoothies, ice cream, or even watermelon salad. More famously, mint is also used to make jelly traditionally served with lamb. Another plus is that growing mint near your back door or kitchen windowsill serves as a great deterrent for ants, flies, and mosquitoes.

- **Thyme:** As another perennial, thyme is famous for being able to withstand a range of different climates and varying soil conditions. It's this combination that makes it an excellent choice for a first-time gardener. Both fresh and dried thyme can enhance any chicken and lamb dish.

- **Chives:** With their hardy nature, chives are another herb that's super easy to grow. Aside from requiring minimal care, chives are famous for adding a gentle onion flavor to many different dishes. The most popular are stir-fries and even Asian dishes. Chives are also an excellent addition to anti-inflammatory medicines.

## GATHERING YOUR GARDENING TOOLS: THE ESSENTIALS

As with just about anything else, the success of your garden boils down to using the right tools to get the job done. To make the whole gardening process so much easier, it's necessary to invest in a few key essentials. Fortunately, tending an herb garden doesn't require fancy gadgets and complex tools. My garden has grown considerably, and I still only use the basic tools I started with! Here's a list of my go-to herbing tools:

- **Gardening gloves**: Some of the weeds that grow around your herbs may have thorns, especially in outdoor gardens. Opt for a pair of quality gloves to ensure your hands stay clean and thorn-free. For outdoor gardens, you'll need to invest in a sun hat as well.
- **Hand rakes:** For the most part, hand rakes are great for raking away small stones, leaves, and even clearing weeds in container pots and especially outdoor gardens. For bigger garden spaces, I suggest investing in a standard-size leaf rake as well. It will be so much easier to rake up the leaves and keep your garden tidy.
- **Trowels:** Essentially, trowels are those small handheld spades that can be used to dig holes and even remove stubborn weeds. As with the rakes, bigger options are better suited to larger gardens.

- **Watering can or hose with light spray option:**
  As with the other tools, whether you use a
  watering can or a hose will depend on the size and
  location of your garden. For instance, you aren't
  going to water a massive backyard garden with a
  watering can! You also aren't going to water your
  windowsill pots with the hose. For windowsill
  pots, you can also use a simple spray bottle to
  spritz your herbs. It's essential to keep your herbs
  hydrated without damaging their sensitive leaves.
  Keep in mind that a strong spray of water will
  wash away the soil.
- **Herb scissor set:** When it's time to harvest your
  herbs, a simple herb scissor set will be ideal. You'll
  also use this scissor set for pruning.

*Preparing Your Gardening Space: Laying the Foundation*

As with building, laying a good foundation is essential for
a healthy and successful herb garden. When you're
creating your herb garden foundation, follow these
important tips.

**Outdoors**

1. Decide on the most suitable spot for your garden.
2. Assess the number of herbs you want to grow—if
   you're hesitant about taking on a large garden
   right from the beginning, start with a small patch
   that you can manage easily.

3. Prepare the area by removing any grass, weeds, and other shrubs.

4. Use your trowel or spade to loosen the soil. If you aren't convinced of the health of your soil, remember to start with a pH test. You can buy a testing kit at your local garden center.

5. If you're ready to plant, create planting holes about twice the width of the root of your herbling. Leave enough space between plants so that they can spread out and grow properly. You also need to work in your garden, so add some working room between your plants.

**Container Garden**

1. Choose strong containers that can handle the weight of the soil as well as the addition of regular watering.

2. Add drainage holes to the pots—as I mentioned in Chapter 1, simply drill a few ½ to 1-inch holes around the surface of the container, depending upon the overall container size.

3. Add a planter tray under each container to ensure that all the water, nutrients and soil don't leak out all over your courtyard or balcony.

4. Choose a well-draining potting mix. While there are several brands I could recommend, I suggest you speak to your local gardening center. That will prevent me from sending you running around

for a soil mix that may not be available in your area. Be sure to specify to the consultants at the gardening center that you need the soil for container herb gardening.

5. Set your containers up in the area where they are going to stand before filling them up with soil— they can be quite heavy to carry around once filled. Especially if you're opting for larger pots!

**Windowsill**

1. If possible, pick the most south-facing windowsill to ensure maximum sunlight.
2. Where only a section of your little herbling gets light, I suggest rotating your pots a few times a week so that all sides of the plant get sunlight exposure.
3. Ensure the pots and their trays fit properly in the windowsill to avoid them getting knocked over.
4. Ensure your windowsill containers have adequate drainage holes.
5. For soil, follow step 4 in the above container section.
6. Invest in a grow light if your windowsill doesn't get the necessary sun in the winter months.

## Vertical

1. Decide on the wall you're going to use—where possible, choose one that gets the most sunlight for the longest period during the day.
2. Secure a trellis panel or metal frame onto the wall —this will support a few different-sized pots.
3. You can also place sheeting against the wall. That means your pots will be against the sheeting rather than directly against the wall. This will prevent any water damage to the wall—ideal for instances where you're using a balcony or porch wall.
4. Have an irrigation system in mind—as a beginner, it may be easier to start with a spray bottle and watering can. As your gardening skills develop, you can opt for a more complicated but effective irrigation system.
5. If you're opting for a vertical planter system from your garden center, you'll notice that they all share a similar concept for water drainage. The top pot drains into the second and lower levels. You then just add a tray at the bottom to avoid the last pot becoming waterlogged. Keep this design in mind if you're using your own pots to create a vertical design. It's a good idea to place a planter at the bottom of the last pot to avoid having water draining straight down onto the balcony floor all day.

*Planting Your Herbs: The Birth of Your Garden*

You owe it to your little herblings to give them the strongest start if you want them to flourish and turn you into a successful herb gardener.

To ensure that you give your herblings the best start, I urge you to follow these simple but effective tips:

1. If you're planting seeds from a seed packet, always follow the listed instructions. This will help you get the planting depth and spacing correct.
2. For little seedlings or young herblings, dig a hole that's both wide and deep enough to accommodate the root.
3. Place the little herblings inside their holes and gently fill them with soil. This applies to any gardening method you're opting for.
4. Be sure to find out how much space each herb needs to grow by checking how big that particular herb usually gets. The mature size is often listed on a seed packet.
5. Avoid overcrowding, as this can lead to weaker plants and can also increase the risk of disease. Close proximity also means that your little herbs will be fighting for the same nutrients and sunlight.
6. I can't stress this enough—ensure that you have correct drainage to eliminate root rot and drowning.

7. The number of times you water your garden depends on the temperature in your backyard. For indoor plants, consider factors such as humidity and pot type. For the most part, herbs require water two to three times a week.

8. When choosing a fertilizer, always opt for a slow-releasing variant for instances where you're using sandy soil. This is because nutrients tend to wash out quickly with this soil type. To give your herbs an extra boost, consider adding fish emulsion because it's organic and high in nitrogen.

### *Caring for Your New Garden: The First Few Weeks*

Taking care of your little herblings is about more than simply getting them in the ground. The first few weeks are essential to getting them used to their environment. To do this, follow these simple tips:

1. Monitor your little plants for early signs of disease —wilting or discolored leaves.

2. Look out for pests that may have transferred from other plants in the garden. Remember that early detection makes treatment more effective.

3. For indoor herbs, it's a good idea to rotate your pots every few days in the first few weeks. This will ensure that all sides of your herblings get equal exposure to the available sunlight.

4. Check your plants to ensure that they are draining correctly. Adjust your watering routine as needed.

*Consider the Pots You Use for Your Indoor Herbs*

You may think that choosing the best pots for your windowsill herbs is all about matching your decor or trying to create a rustic garden feel. However, you may be surprised to learn that some pot materials are actually better for your little herblings than others. Consider the pointers listed below.

- **Plastic (such as repurposed food containers):** Since plastic pots retain moisture for longer periods, they are instantly better suited to herbs that prefer damper soil. Keep in mind that if you're repurposing an old container that you intend on painting, opt for organic paint and don't paint the inside of the pot. You wouldn't want paint chemicals leaching into the soil. Remember to drill a few drainage holes.
- **Metal:** Whether you're buying metal pots or repurposing an old coffee tin, keep in mind that these pots retain heat, which in turn dries out the soil. If you're going to use metal pots, be sure to increase your watering schedule to compensate for the soil drying out. Alternatively, use metal containers for pots that prefer dry soil. Once

again, remember the drainage holes for repurposed pots.

- **Wood:** Sometimes wood as a plant container can be tricky. Ideally, you don't want to use wood that has been treated with chemicals such as varnish or lacquer as this may look shiny, but the chemicals will leach into the soil—a big no-no for soil that's growing anything you want to eat. If you want to use wood, opt for the untreated kind. Here you want to keep in mind that wood retains water, making it an excellent option for herbs that prefer moist conditions. Depending on the quality of the wood, you may need to replace your pots after a while as the wood breaks down from the constant moisture. Also, keep an eye out for wood-boring pests such as termites.

- **Ceramic:** Gardeners love ceramic pots because of their stylish look, and I always feel that using them makes me look like a gardener who knows what they're doing! However, I want to point out that they retain moisture, making them excellent for herbs that require moist soil. They are also better suited to warmer climates.

- **Clay/terracotta:** If you live in cooler climates, you may want to consider clay or terracotta pots. They're porous, which allows for better air movement. That in turn means they dry out faster. Watch the water levels if you're going to use these pots.

It's worth pointing out that some herbs grow faster than others, so, it's not unusual to see some types shooting up while others seem to take longer to get growing. Don't give up on the slow growers, just keep nurturing them— they'll get there!

The first few weeks of your little herblings' lives are also the time you'll need to master the watering, light, and fertilizer requirements of each specific herb. Fortunately, the next chapter will help you get a handle on all three of these aspects. And, contrary to those difficult herb-growing manuals, it's actually easier than you think!

# 4

# QUENCHING THIRST, BASKING IN LIGHT, AND NOURISHING ROOTS: YOUR HERBS BASIC NEEDS

*As for rosemary, I let it run all over my garden walls, not only because my bees love it but because it is the herb sacred to remembrance and to friendship, whence a sprig of it hath a dumb language.*

— THOMAS MOORE

W hile all herbs are plants, it's important to note that they require different levels of water, sunlight, and nutrients. One of the top reasons first-time gardeners struggle is that they tend to treat all herbs the same.

Having an understanding of what your herb of choice's watering, light preferences, and favorite nutrients are, will go a long way toward making the growing process so much more successful. With that in mind, let's take a look at some of the more significant preferences.

## WATERING WISDOM: WHEN AND HOW MUCH?

Watering your new little herblings is a little more complex than just pouring a glass of water over them every time you pass by the kitchen windowsill. I've compiled a few easy-to-follow tips that will help you avoid watering too much or too little, especially in the early days of your herb gardening journey. Furthermore, I've included a brief look at the best watering techniques to help you make the process as easy as possible.

### Watering Tips for Herbs

Whether you're growing your herbs from little plants or germinating seeds directly in the ground, it's a good idea to keep the following tips in mind as you establish a watering routine.

1. **Do not water herbs the same as houseplants:** If you've ever grown or looked after a houseplant, you may think there's no difference between them and herbs. However, as I've already mentioned, some herbs can be sensitive to certain watering levels. Be sure to check the seed packet or refer to the table later in this chapter for a guideline on how much water to give each herb.

2. **Water early in the morning:** Successful herb gardening is about the routine. This means watering them at a time when the water can be absorbed rather than dried out in the hot sun. It's always a good idea to water your herblings early in the morning—preferably when the sun is just rising. Avoid watering plants when the sun is at its fullest, as this will cause the water to evaporate before it reaches the root. Dry roots will be the end of your little herblings.

3. **Water around the herb, not all over:** Herbs, for the most part, don't appreciate being showered with water. That means, opt to water around the herb rather than creating a shower effect from the top. Avoid getting water all over the leaves as this can increase the potential onset of mold and mildew. Continuously wet leaves may also develop rot, which will cause your herb to wilt and die.

4. **Use a plant tray:** I always recommend using a plant tray (it's that little saucer that comes with

store-bought pots). These trays serve two essential purposes. The first is to prevent water from draining out of the pot or container all over the windowsill or area around the container. Secondly, they are great for keeping the roots hydrated for longer. The water pools in the tray and the roots and soil *suck* it up through the drainage holes. If the tray is full, discard the water after about 20 minutes to avoid creating root rot. The roots will soak up enough water in those 20 minutes to sustain them for a day or two.

5. **Mulch often:** Mulching is an excellent way to retain soil moisture, which means you can get away with watering less. Here you want to use natural mulching materials such as pine needles, wood chips, and even cocoa bean shells.

### *Watering Techniques to Consider*

When it comes to watering techniques to consider, I often recommend that novice gardeners start with a watering can or even a spray bottle. This is often the easiest way not to become overwhelmed with the whole process in the beginning. As your confidence grows and you prove to yourself that you have what it takes to grow herbs, you may want to move on to a more streamlined irrigation system.

Keep in mind that investing in pipes and gadgets can be costly if you're working on a budget. However, there are a few DIY watering techniques you can consider if you don't want to just rely on remembering to water your herbs.

- **Drip irrigation system**

There are various ways to set up a drip irrigation system. The simplest involves a plastic bottle while more complex outdoor drip irrigation systems can involve setting up pipes and gutters. It all depends on the space of your herb garden and how much you want to invest in it. The biggest advantage of a drip irrigation system is that it reduces water usage because the goal is to target the root zone directly rather than wasting water on areas that won't benefit the plant.

I want to share a simple DIY drip irrigation system with you that you can add to your indoor plants. On a larger scale, it can work for larger outdoor containers and even backyard herb gardens. This is how:

- **Step 1: Gather your equipment:** You'll need a clean, empty drinking bottle such as a soda or water bottle, as well as a sharp pair of scissors and a cotton swab.
- **Step 2: Poke a small hole in the side of the bottle and the top of the lid:** Ideally, the hole should be about two inches from the bottom of the bottle, making it wide enough for the stem of

cotton to fit in. You'll want to do the same for the plastic lid.

- **Step 3: Cut the cotton swab in half and fit it into the bottle:** Insert each end into one of the holes. The fluffy end of the swab should be on the outside of the bottle. This will create a water delivery system where the water leaks out slowly from the bottom bud. The top bud controls the water flow. Leaving the top bud in will allow the water to drip out more slowly. If you need a quicker water flow for days when the soil seems drier, simply take the bud out and let the water flow faster. You can let the water run through the bottle at a faster rate for a few minutes to create moist soil and then pop the top swab back in to slow the water to a drip rather than a flow that could drown the herblings.

- **Step 4: Fill the bottle with water:** Use a jug or glass to fill your bottle once you have it positioned in place. If you're adding fertilizer mixed with water, you can mix it beforehand and pour it into the bottle to drip into the ground. To save water, consider using gray water. That means using bath water, washing machine water, and even rain-harvested water. You can use any water that doesn't contain harsh chemicals. Also, never use wastewater from the toilet. Reusing your water is another step in creating a sustainable herb garden.

- **Step 5: Place the bottle in the pot plant or garden bed:** Keep in mind that you should always use a pot that's proportionate to the expected size of your herb. Be wary of using a pot that's too big as this will have a lot of wasted soil that will drain water that isn't needed. Typically, the right size pot should allow you ample space to slot the bottle in the pot next to the herbling. You can make a little trench to bed the bottle into the soil.

Here, you want the tip of the cotton swab to reach just above the soil surface, to maintain the drip function. Planting the bottle is also good for keeping it in place when there's a gush of wind, making it great for outdoor containers. Choose a bottle that isn't too big for your space/pot/container.

- **Soaker hose**

If you're not too convinced about the effectiveness of a water bottle planted next to your herblings, then a soaker hose may be more effective. This type of irrigation may also be more effective for larger herb gardens.

Soaker hoses are simple garden hoses with holes that lie flat on the ground. Unlike sprinklers and sprayers, soaker hoses enable you to water directly to the ground, which is perfect for herbs. They also avoid getting leaves wet.

Soaker hoses distribute the water slowly and more evenly through your soil rather than pooling on the surface.

Since soaker hoses can be easily moved, or left in place as a regular watering system, they can be more effective than hand watering. Most herbs will benefit from about 30 minutes twice a week through the soaker hose. You can pick up a soaker hose at any garden center or hardware store. Stores such as Lowes and Walmart usually stock them as well.

### Signs of Overwatering to Watch Out For

It's easy to unintentionally overwater your herblings in the beginning, especially when the ground looks dry or you're not seeing the results as often as you anticipate. However, overwatering is a sure herb killer in most instances.

Here are a few signs that you may be overwatering your herbs:

- fuzzy
- weak stems that break easily
- yellowing leaves
- herbs aren't growing
- abnormally soft roots
- heavier than usual leaf fall

If your herbs haven't died by the time you realize you may be overwatering, it's as simple as reducing your current watering routine. Allow the soil a day or two to dry up to a moist level rather than a drenched level. Prune the yellow leaves and wipe off any possible moldy spots. Rotate pots in the sun to increase the rate at which the water evaporates until the soil is no longer drenched. From then on, only give the plant water just before the soil is dry, and be sure to not overwater.

## SOAKING UP THE SUN: THE IMPORTANCE OF LIGHT

The right amount of light is essential for proper growth. Additionally, energy from the sun's rays powers photosynthesis, and this, in turn, creates the food needed to fuel plant growth, bloom, and produce seeds for future plants. That said, there's a delicate balance of light that should be achieved because too much sun can be as damaging as too little light.

As I've mentioned before, most herbs require at least six hours of full sun every day. There are a few that can grow in more shady areas, though. That makes knowing what you want to grow important as you start sourcing the best spot for your herb garden. Let's take a look at the definition of light stress, as well as knowing the signs of too much or too little light.

**Be Wary of Light Stress**

Light stress refers to the detrimental effect that constant exposure to excess or insufficient light levels has on your little herblings. Either one of these instances can affect the photosynthetic activity. Both instances can stunt plant growth and eventually render your herb unfruitful.

Let's take a look at the signs.

**Signs of Too Much Light**

- **Leaves that appear sun-bleached or faded:** Severe sunlight causes much-needed chlorophyll to break down in the leaf. Pale, bleached, and faded leaves are a clear sign that this is happening.
- **Brittle leaves:** When chlorophyll breaks down, the leaves become brown and brittle and break easily.
- **Excessively dry soil:** If the soil seems excessively dry, no matter how often you're watering, it could be a sign that there's too much light and heat radiating down on the plants.

To reduce sun exposure, remove the indoor pots from the windowsill for a few hours every day. Be sure to put them in an area where they'll still get adequate but less harsh light. For outdoor herbs, it may be a good idea to place four poles around the herb garden and place a light garden netting or shading over the poles, forming a sort of canopy.

This will help reduce harsh sunlight from scorching your herblings. Be sure to remove the netting as soon as the sun moves away from the garden. To avoid this hassle every day, be sure to take the sunlight into consideration when you're choosing a location. Alternatively, you can build a mini greenhouse over your outdoor garden when your herbs start growing.

**Signs of Too Little Light**

- **Long spaces on the stems between the leaf nodes:** This is the point where the leaves grow out from the stem and ideally they should be close together.
- **Excessive leaf fall:** Herbs with insufficient light will drop their leaves more often, even in the summer months.
- **Wrong color:** Too little light will also cause your herbling to be a pale yellow or brown color. Remember that a healthy herb plant should always be a rich green color, with vibrant and strong leaves and stems.

If you suspect your little herb may be suffering from too little light, move indoor plants to a different location. Alternatively, you can invest in a grow light that will provide sufficient light during low light times of the day.

For outdoor herbs, ensure that there are no trees or shrubs that may be creating shade over your herbs. Before planting your herbs in the backyard or other outdoor areas, be sure to check how much light shines in that area during a full day. A lack of adequate sunlight is often the reason why many gardeners forgo the idea of a backyard garden for a container or windowsill option. After all, pots and containers are easier to move to a newer, sunnier spot if necessary.

## FEEDING YOUR HERBS: NUTRIENT NEEDS AND ORGANIC FERTILIZERS

Essentially, most herbs need a considerable amount of phosphorous, potassium, and nitrogen to grow into the strong and healthy plants you're striving for. The easiest way to give your herblings a head start is to ensure that they are planted in the healthiest soil. To increase nutrients, consider adding a fertilizer rich in the particular nutrient your soil is lacking (a soil test from your garden center will help you determine this).

The nutrient levels in store-bought fertilizer can be found on the package and will be labeled as the NPK (nitrogen, phosphorous, potassium) value. For the most part, herbs prefer an NPK ratio of 4-1-1 or 5-1-1. The good news is that you can choose a fertilizer that's stronger in the nutrients your soil is lacking to create the perfect boost without providing too much of the other nutrients. So, when buying fertilizer, your garden center agent may ask you what you're growing and what nutrient you're looking to improve. A general fertilizer will be balanced and will provide an overall infusion of these three nutrients.

### When Should You Add Fertilizer?

Typically, fertilizer should be applied in the early spring, as this is the time your herbs start their active growth. You can add another dose in midsummer to give them a boost. Container-grown herbs won't need fertilizer in the winter since plant growth is much slower as a result of shorter days.

The telltale signs that your herbs require fertilizer are that they start withering or even shrinking one or two weeks after they peak in their first growing cycle. Another clear sign is an unusually low pH level—typically less than 5.

### Tips to Avoid Overfertilizing

Many novice gardeners make the mistake of assuming that fertilizer is a must-add to every pot or container. While it's true that herbs, like other plants, need nutrients to grow, it's important to remember that overfertilizing can cause more harm than good. This is especially the case if you're already planting your herbs in a nutrient-rich backyard.

Overfertilizing can often lead to excessive growth but dilute the true flavor of the herbs. To know if you're over-fertilizing, consider these simple tips:

- If you're not sure of the soil quality, speak to your local garden center for a simple soil test, or test the pH.
- If you're opting for store-bought fertilizer, be sure to follow the recommended application rates and timings to prevent overfertilization.
- Always follow the manufacturer's package instructions until you're familiar with what works for your particular soil type.
- Where possible, consider using organic fertilizer.

### *Why Is Organic Fertilizer Better?*

Organic fertilizers are those types that don't contain any harmful chemicals. These types of fertilizers not only boost your plants but also improve the general health of the soil. Unlike inorganic fertilizers, organic variants also improve water movement throughout the soil. They also don't make crusty layers on top of the soil as chemical-rich fertilizers often do.

Furthermore, organic fertilizers are eco-friendly and align with the values associated with organic gardening. The lack of chemicals enhances plant biodiversity and also benefits the microbes already living in your soil's own ecosystem.

Some of the top organic fertilizer options to consider include the following:

- worm castings
- compost made of organic materials, such as kitchen waste (vegetable peels mostly) and grass clippings
- seaweed extract
- fish emulsion
- bone meal
- chicken manure
- cottonseed meal

Check with your local garden center about the types of organic fertilizers they have on hand. In many instances, you can buy small packets for windowsill pots, or larger quantities for container or backyard gardening. Keep in mind that a little goes a long way, so a full bag should really last you quite some time!

### The Best Ways to Apply Fertilizer to Herbs

Once you've decided on what type of fertilizer you're going to use, here's how you should apply it:

1. Work the fertilizer into the top of the soil. This will make it easier for the roots to absorb their nutrients slowly over a longer period of time. Be careful not to place fertilizer directly onto the

roots, as this could burn them, especially if you're opting for inorganic options.

2. Some fertilizer can easily be mixed with water and sprayed onto the top of the soil, to soak down.

3. Be careful to not spray inorganic variants on the herb leaves, as this is the part of the plant that you're going to cook with.

### Breakdown of What Specific Herbs Need

Since I've already mentioned that not all herbs have the same requirements, here's a quick overview of what some of the more common herbs prefer.

| Type of Herb | Light Required | Soil Type | Watering Needs |
| --- | --- | --- | --- |
| Basil | Full sun | Damp and moist | Medium |
| Rosemary | Full sun | Dry | Medium |
| Oregano | Partial sun | Well-drained | Low to medium |
| Sage | Full sun | Dry | Medium |
| Thyme | Full to partial sun | Well-drained | Medium |
| Parsley | Full to partial sun | Well-drained | Low to medium |
| Mint | Full to partial sun | Damp and moist | Medium to high |
| Dill | Full sun | Moist | Medium |
| Cilantro | Full to partial sun | Well-drained | Medium |
| Chives | Full to partial sun | well-drained | Medium |

- **Full sun:** Six to eight hours of light. Rotate windowsill pots to ensure light is evenly spread.
- **Full to partial sun:** Four to six hours of light.
- **Well-drained:** Add a layer of rocks and twigs to the pot before adding soil to increase drainage.
- **Damp and moist:** Soil should never be dry as roots need to remain moist but not soaked. The drip watering system is a great way to keep the soil moist, especially if you don't have a lot of time for watering regularly.
- **Low water:** These herbs should be watered only one day per week.
- **Medium water:** For the most part, these herbs need to be watered twice per week.
- **High watering:** Three to four times per week, as herbs with this water requirement don't like dry soil.

By now you should have a better idea of the importance of mastering the right combination of watering, light, and fertilizer needs. Since herbs are really simple to grow, the good news is that getting this combination right is easier than you think—especially if you have chosen the perfect spot to begin with!

Next on the journey to a healthy and bountiful herb garden is a clearer understanding of providing organic pests and managing disease. The right strategies will not only maintain the health of your herblings but also ensure that you don't add contaminated herbs to your recipes. Keep reading!

## No Mistake Is Wasted

*There are no gardening mistakes, only experiments.*

— JANET KILBURN PHILLIPS

I'd like to remind you at this point that I once thought I didn't have a green thumb... not even a greenish one! I drowned several poor herblings, and I messed up with over-enthusiastic harvesting. Mistakes happen: That's how we learn. But it's my hope that I've made most of the mistakes for you, and this book will help you avoid having to make them yourself.

Nonetheless, sometimes things go wrong, so I'd like to remind you of my story so that you don't get disheartened if they do. Keep persevering; keep following the advice you're finding here. You will get there, and eventually, you'll look back at your mistakes as teaching points that helped you get to your thriving herb garden.

So many people get put off by those early mistakes, and I'm on a mission to make sure that doesn't happen – by seeing that beginner gardeners start out with all the information they need to avoid falling over at the first hurdle.

Since you've joined me on my mission and you're already well on your way to an abundant herb garden, I'd like to ask for your help in reaching more new gardeners. All that will take is a few moments of your time and a short review.

**By leaving a review of this book on Amazon, you'll help other new gardeners find all the herb gardening guidance they need to see success without encountering the pitfalls.**

It doesn't matter that we make mistakes... as long as we don't let them put us off. But if we can reduce the chances of them happening from the get-go, we'll see a world with more happy gardeners and more thriving herb gardens.

Thank you so much for your support. Herbs in gardens everywhere will thank you!

**Scan the QR code below to leave your review!**

# 5

# GUARDIAN OF THE GARDEN: ORGANIC PEST AND DISEASE MANAGEMENT

*The glory of gardening: hands in the dirt, head in the sun, heart with nature. To nurture a garden is to feed not just the body, but the soul.*

— ALFRED AUSTIN

Just about everyone who grows herbs does so for the nutritional value and flavor they add to any recipe. Even herbs that aren't for eating, such as lavender, are used for the benefits they offer the human body. With that in mind, your number one goal should always be to grow the healthiest plants possible.

The number one way to do this is to understand potential pest and disease risks as well as a few strategies to effectively deal with them. This chapter takes a more in-depth look at the top pests to look out for, the more effective ways of dealing with disease, and, of course, the best steps to keep pesky little critters out of your herb pots, containers, or outdoor gardens.

## IDENTIFYING THE USUAL SUSPECTS: COMMON PESTS IN HERB GARDENS

It has to be said: Every gardener, whether novice or seasoned, will have to deal with pests at some point in their gardening journey. Effectively dealing with bugs and pests starts by knowing what they are and how to identify them. Let's take a look at the more prominent suspects to keep an eye out for.

### Aphids

- **Characteristic:** These pesky little creatures are attracted to tender new leaves. They're commonly found among crowded and healthy herbs. In some instances, they're white in color, making them relatively easy to spot. The green varieties can make it difficult to notice them, though, unless you're doing a thorough leaf check.

- **Signs to look out for**: Clear signs include curling foliage as well as a sooty mold all over the plant that attracts ants. Since they suck crucial plant juice out of your herbs, you'll also notice your herb leaves turning yellow and that your plant will stop growing.

### *Spider Mites*

- **Characteristics:** Spider mites prefer dry, hot conditions, and eat various herbs. They can be found on both your indoor and outdoor plants and are often attracted to the mulch you've put around your plants. If you suspect your herbs may have mites, consider changing your mulch to wood chips.
- **Signs to look out for:** These little mites can be seen on the underside of herb leaves and can be washed off with a strong stream of water. Be sure to dry the leaves afterward.

## Leafhoppers

- **Characteristics:** They are commonly found in parsley, basil, and oregano. For the most part, they're brightly colored and tend to jump when disturbed. Since they're mostly found in warmer regions, it's a good idea to do extra checks if you live in the sunnier regions of the US.
- **Signs to look out for:** Leaves infected with leafhoppers usually turn yellow before brown and then curling and wilting. There may also be signs of black sooty mold growing on the leaf surface.

## Slugs and Snails

- **Characteristics:** They usually come out at night to feed on outdoor herb plants.
- **Signs to look out for:** The first signs include large holes in your herb leaves or stems. You'll also see slimy trails across your herbs as well as on the ground surrounding the plant.

## Whiteflies

- **Characteristics:** These are tiny, winged pests that are usually covered with a white wax.
- **Signs to look out for:** Whiteflies can be found on the underside of leaves and cause damage to herbs by feeding on the plant's sap.

## *Leaf Miners*

- **Characteristics:** Leaf miners are typically small brown bugs that are attracted to succulent basil leaves.
- **Signs to look out for:** They're easy to spot as you'll see tunneling trails across the upper and lower leaves.

## *Flea Beetles*

- **Characteristics:** Commonly found in vegetable patches, flea beetles are small, shiny, and can jump!
- **Signs to look out for:** They chew irregular-sized holes in the leaves of otherwise healthy herbs. Keep an eye out for soft fluffy larvae as they lay their eggs on the leaves.

## *Parsley Worms*

- **Characteristics:** Many people tend to ignore parsley worms on their herbs as they start out as green and black swallowtail caterpillars that morph into butterflies.
- **Signs to look out for:** They often appear on parsley (hence the name), dill, and fennel. They may chew some leaves on your herbs but won't destroy the plant. Rather than kill something that

turns into a butterfly, opt to relocate the caterpillar or in more severe cases, invest in a few row covers (little white tent-like domes that you can put over the plant)

### Spittlebugs

- **Characteristics:** These are brown bugs that are capable of jumping to many times their height and length. They are typically found all over your garden and don't have a preferred herb. The spit that they secrete can halt plant production.
- **Signs to look out for:** The most obvious sign that you're dealing with a spittlebug is the spit-like froth they leave behind on the plant leaves and stems.

### Weevils

- **Characteristics:** Weevils are easy to spot as they have elongated snouts. You may recognize them from your pantry where they often invade stored foods to lay eggs. Out in your garden, they leave distinctive and irregularly shaped bite marks on the leaf margins of your little herblings.
- **Signs to look out for:** Look out for them on your carrots and parsley. The floury dust that they leave behind is a dead giveaway that they're in your garden.

## NOT JUST A BUG'S LIFE: DEALING WITH DISEASE

It's important to acknowledge that your little herblings aren't only at risk of being attacked by pests but can also fall victim to a host of different diseases. Side effects of these diseases can affect the herb plant's growth as well as their yield.

Some of the diseases that can commonly appear on indoor or outdoor herbs are listed below.

| Name of Disease | Signs to Look Out For | Common Causes |
| --- | --- | --- |
| Powdery mildew | A fungal disease that appears as a white powdery coating on leaves and can stunt your herblings growth. | Typically caused by hot and humid weather. |
| Downy mildew | Also a fungal disease that shows up as yellow spots on the tops of your herbling leaves. Can also present as a purple, fuzzy mold on the undersides of the leaves. | Usually happens in continuous cool and wet conditions. |
| Root rot | Causes herbs to wilt and turn yellow. Roots turn brown and become mushy, rather than being healthy, firm, and white. | Primarily caused by overwatering. |
| Soluble salt injury | Herbs show signs of root injury and may first appear as though the plant has root rot. White crystalline deposits appear around the edges of the herb pot or container. | Caused by excessive fertilization, as high levels of soluble salt accumulate in the pots, containers, or ground area within the range of the herbs. |

Keep in mind that these are just a few of the many potential diseases you could find on your herblings. This is why I urge you to regularly check your herblings. Run your fingers over the leaves to test for mold, look out for fuzzy white dots, and don't forget that holes in your herb leaves and stems are a clear indication that there's a problem. Fortunately, there are a few things you can do to reduce the effect of diseases and bugs on your precious little herblings.

## A BUG'S NIGHTMARE: ORGANIC PEST CONTROL METHODS

If your goal is to keep your garden as organic as possible, then you'll want to opt for organic pest control methods. While it may be tempting to reach for the strongest pesticide your garden center has, be warned that this will affect the safety of plants that you are hoping to add to your food at some point.

Some of the more effective organic pest control methods to consider are listed below.

1. **Beneficial insects:** Outdoor herb gardens will benefit from introducing insects such as ladybugs and lacewings to the area. This is because they're natural predators of pests such as aphids. The good news is that you don't have to hunt for ladybugs to include in your garden. Simply attract

them by planting sunflowers and marigolds near your herbs. You can do this in containers around the herb pots or even around the edges of your outdoor herb garden. On the plus side, you'll be adding color and fragrance to your garden as well.

2. **Organic sprays:** Ideally, you want to kill the pests without harming or poisoning the herbs. Harsh pesticides will not only harm the plants but may also kill the beneficial pests (such as the ladybugs). Rather, opt for organic sprays such as neem oil or insecticidal soap. Both products can be purchased from your local garden center, Home Depot, or even ordered online from retail outlets such as Amazon.

3. **Physical barriers:** You can also create or install a physical barrier around your herb garden or on the edge of the containers. Common organic options include copper tape and eggshells—these will deter snails and slugs as they try to cross over into the garden.

4. **Plant companion plants that deter pests:** As I mentioned in Chapter 1, there are many plants that you can plant next to—or very near to—your herbs to not only provide support but also deter pests. For instance, garlic is excellent for deterring fungus gnats, cabbage loppers, and spider mites. Catnip, on the other hand, is great for keeping aphids and ticks away while basil helps keep tomato hookworms out of your herb area. Other

herbs such as lavender also deter pests that eat herbs as well as household pests such as cockroaches and ants.

5. **Adding onions:** Yes, I know, onions are vegetables, and this is an herb garden we're trying to grow here, but, these fragrant alliums are a natural enemy to bugs such as aphids and snails. If you have no purpose for the onions themselves, you can opt for the ornamental variety which won't require harvesting. Scattering them throughout your garden will not only keep the bugs at bay but also add a wonderful pop of color to your herb garden. For container gardens, plant one or two pots close to the herbs that are prone to aphids. For outdoor gardens, I recommend scattering them throughout the garden.

## DON'T LET IT SPREAD: ORGANIC DISEASE MANAGEMENT

Finding signs of disease in your garden, windowsill, or containers can be very stressful, as you may start thinking you have failed at your herb gardening before it's even begun! Well, it's important to note that even the most seasoned gardener will at some point have to deal with plant disease. In some cases, disease can be devastating and even fatal to your herblings. However, there are a few pointers I'd like to share that can help you keep the most common diseases in check.

1. **Crop rotation:** The concept of crop rotation refers to not planting the same herb in the same spot year after year. That means that after harvesting, it's a good idea to plant the new seeds or the little herblings in a new spot. Doing this prevents diseases from building up in the soil. Moving the plant enables you to treat that particular part of the soil with fertilizer. It's also an opportunity to test the pH of that spot. You can use a gardening app such as GrowVeg to help you plan your rotation schedule.

2. **Proper air circulation:** If you have a small backyard space, you might be tempted to plant your herbs as close together as possible to get the most herbs possible. However, this isn't always the best idea. Space out your herbs to prevent fungal diseases from rubbing off one herb's leaves to another. For herbs that are planted close together, be sure to keep them pruned after checking them regularly.

3. **Organic fungicides:** If you find signs of a fungal disease, I recommend using organic fungicides such as copper spray or even baking soda to safely treat the herblings. You can either buy these from your Home Depot or simply make them at home by mixing water with baking soda in a spray bottle. Since baking soda is safe to consume, it's not harmful to the herbs and won't affect your recipes!

PREVENTION IS THE BEST CURE:
MAINTAINING PLANT HEALTH

The adage *prevention is better than cure* comes to mind when it's time to discuss plant health. As with your health, it's always better to prevent your herblings from getting a disease than it is trying to get rid of a potential garden-destroying fungus! Here are a few tips that will help you maintain your herbling's plant health:

1. **Proper watering:** Be sure to water your herbs properly. This means watering deeply but less frequently. It's a sure way to prevent common diseases such as root rot. This method of watering also makes your herbs more drought tolerant.
2. **Opting for organic fertilizers:** Avoid harsh chemical fertilizers as they can weaken your herbs, making them more susceptible to disease. Instead, opt for worm castings and compost to keep the herblings strong. You can also make your own compost to ensure you're using the most natural options.
3. **Checking your herbs regularly:** It's easy to notice disease if you're watering a few windowsill pots, but it may be less obvious if you have a bigger backyard garden that you're watering with a hose. Be sure to take time to check each herb and the surrounding soil. Signs may include fuzzy mold, yellowing leaves, and weak stems. Early

detection may be the difference between saving your herblings and having to start all over again. Keep in mind that plant disease can spread, so dealing with the ill herbling can prevent the illness from spreading to other plants.

4. **Cleaning your tools:** If you're using your garden tools regularly, it's essential to wash or sterilize them after each use. This may sound a bit extreme, but pruning a diseased plant can transfer fungus or bacteria to your tools. This in turn can spread the bacteria to your other herbs, which can be catastrophic if you're getting ready to use those tools to harvest your first herblings!

Keeping your little herblings disease-free may seem like it's complex and a lot of work. But once you get started with your herb garden, you'll see that it's easier than you thought. The secret is to check them for early signs of pest activity or disease. The earlier you spot the problem, the quicker you'll be able to stop it from spreading and deal with the problem.

Once you manage to get your herbs to adulthood, they'll be ready for harvesting. It's essential to understand how they should be harvested and stored as this will ensure that they can be used the way you intended. Read on for some tips on successful harvesting!

# 6

# REAPING THE REWARDS: HARVESTING AND STORING YOUR HERBS

*Gardening with herbs, which is becoming increasingly popular, is indulged in by those who like subtlety in their plants in preference to brilliance.*

— HELEN MORGENTHAU FOX

There's something very satisfying about picking your own herbs and including them in your favorite recipes. This is especially true if you've opted for more aromatic and flavorful herbs such as basil, oregano, sage, and parsley. Perhaps it's because fresh herbs always taste considerably better than the dried versions you get in the supermarket, or it might just have something to do with the satisfaction of growing, nurturing, and cultivating your own little herblings from scratch!

With that said, it's important to note that harvesting and storage techniques are as important as all the other steps that have gotten you to this point. The last thing you want to do at this point is drop the ball during the harvesting process—after all your hard work to get here! If your intention is to cook your herbs, then this chapter is an absolute must-read.

## THE PERFECT TIMING: WHEN TO HARVEST YOUR HERBS

As with the water and light requirements, each type of herb has its own ideal time for harvesting. Knowing when to harvest your herbs will ensure that you pick them when they have the best nutritional content and flavor to offer.

Here is a breakdown of the best harvest times for some of the more common herb choices.

- **Basil:** Your basil should be harvested before it flowers as the essential oil content is at its strongest then. That means it will have the strongest flavor.
- **Thyme:** To harvest thyme, cut off the top five to six inches of growth just before the plant flowers. Don't harvest the tough, woody parts. Be sure to harvest your thyme in the morning, just after the dew has dried. This is when the plant is at its freshest.
- **Mint:** As with most other herbs, mint should be harvested just before flowering. Since mint has a robust flavor profile, you'll want to harvest during this time to take advantage of that great flavor.
- **Rosemary:** While rosemary can be harvested at any time from when leaves start appearing, keep in mind that they're the most flavorful in the early morning after the dew has dried up but before the sun gets too hot.
- **Ginger:** You will have to wait until your ginger plant has reached its full maturity before you can start harvesting it. Picking any before then will damage the plant and cause it to stop growing. Here, you're looking at about eight to ten months. So, if you plant it in the spring, it should be ready to harvest in the winter. The flowering plant that grows from the ginger root must become dry before you harvest it.

- **Cilantro:** Your cilantro plant will be ready when it's about 6 inches tall. The good news is that you don't have to wait for the cilantro plant to be fully grown to harvest the leaves. In fact, you can start harvesting between 45 and 70 days after planting. If you don't want to harvest all your cilantro at once, you can pluck a few individual leaves as you need them. Be sure to do it gently so that you don't damage your herbling.

- **Chives:** Typically, your chive plant will be ready to harvest as soon as the leaves are long enough to clip. Be sure to cut the chives from the outside of the clump, leaving about half an inch of stem behind. This is usually about 60 days after you plant the seeds.

- **Parsley:** For the most part, your parsley plants will be ready for harvesting when they are about 6 inches tall. Make sure that the leaves have at least three separate segments above the ground. Leaves will also be curling.

- **Turmeric:** Typically, turmeric produces rhizomes that are generally ready for harvest in the late fall or early winter. As soon as the plant goes dormant and appears to have stopped growing, it's time to harvest. Since turmeric is a perennial, it dies in the winter, but if you leave the roots intact, the plant will regrow in the late spring.

- **Dill:** Dill can be harvested at any time, provided it's before the plants start flowering. With dill, you'll want to harvest the leaves as these are the most tender part of the plant and are also the most aromatic (unlike the stems or stalks).

- **Sage:** The best time to harvest sage is in the spring and summer as this is the time plants are actively growing. Be sure to harvest them before they flower as they start losing their aroma after flowering.

- **Oregano:** To harvest your oregano plant, wait until the stems have grown to at least 4 to 5 inches tall. You'll want to harvest your oregano just before it blooms.

- **Lavender:** With lavender, there's no need to harvest before the flower buds arrive. Since the buds are the items being harvested, you can wait until 40% to 50% of the plant has flowers, and then harvest them. Cutting your buds off in the spring will mean you can potentially have a second harvest. It's a good idea to harvest when the buds are swollen, and the flowers are starting to open.

- **Chamomile:** The best time to harvest your chamomile flowers is around midday on a sunny day when the flowers are open to the fullest. Flowering time is usually between June and September. Look out for flat petals that fall back from the center of the bud.

### *Be Sure to Understand Your Herb's Growth Cycle*

When it comes to our herbs, it's important to note that it's not as simple as *planting in the winter and harvesting in the spring.* This statement is a common misconception among new gardeners who can see the little herblings being harvested too early. Doing this means you'll end up with leaves, and harvesting isn't so cut and dry because they have different growth cycles. This means you will need to establish the growth cycle of the herbs you've planted.

Typically, the golden rule of annuals and perennials should offer some guidance in this regard.

**Annuals:** Herbs that fall into this category have a fast growth cycle. This means you can harvest them multiple times in one season. Remember that annual herbs need to be replanted every year. Examples of annual herbs include the following:

- basil
- cilantro
- dill
- chamomile
- marjoram
- fennel

**Perennials:** These are the herbs that, if their root system is strongly nurtured, will continue to grow year after year. Since their root system is still developing, they tend to have a slower growth cycle. This means you may need to harvest them sparingly in the first year so that the root system can establish itself. The most common examples of perennial herbs are as follows:

- mint
- thyme
- tarragon
- lavender
- rosemary
- oregano
- sage
- lemon balm

### The Right Technique: How to Harvest Your Herbs

Knowing *when* to harvest your herbs is only half of a successful herb-gathering process. The other half is made up of knowing *what* harvesting technique to opt for. Harvesting your herbs correctly will ensure that they remain as healthy as possible and continue to produce through the remainder of the season.

As with everything else herb related, I have compiled a few tried and trusted tips to help you get started.

1. **Understand your herb type:** Before you reach for the sheers and start cutting wildly, take the time to know which herb you're dealing with and what you're going to do with it. This will help you

estimate how much you need to cut off during the first round. Also, be sure to understand what part of the herb you need. For instance, for leafy herbs such as basil and parsley, you'll need to cut just above a leaf pair. This encourages bushier regrowth. On the other hand, woody herbs like thyme and rosemary need to be snipped off at the top of the stems. With woody stems, you need to be careful not to cut into the actual woody growth as this will hamper regrowth and be the starting point for bacteria.

2. **Always use clean tools:** I discussed the importance of using clean tools in Chapter 5 but will gladly remind you that you should always use clean (and sterilized, if necessary) tools and utensils for harvesting and pruning. Common tools to use include herb or regular garden sheers, kitchen scissors, or even a sharp knife.

3. **Wash your hands**: If you're going to be handling your herblings for harvesting, be sure to wash your hands before you do. This is especially important if you have been handling other plants or veggies. Just as disease and bacteria can spread from your tools, it can also spread from your hands. Hand harvesting, where you break the leaves or flowers off using your hands, is great for soft-stemmed herbs such as mint and basil. Be gentle to avoid damaging your precious little herbling.

## STORING FRESH: HOW TO KEEP YOUR HERBS FRESH

It's very unlikely that you're going to use all your herbs on the first day of harvest unless you're only harvesting one tiny little plant. But, even then, you may need to store the remainder of your precious herblings for them to maintain their flavor and aroma. Fortunately, there are various ways to store your herbs to prolong their shelf life.

For starters, soft herbs such as basil and parsley are among the most commonly used and are great for anything from salads to meat dishes. Simply follow these few easy steps to keep soft herbs as fresh as possible, for as long as possible.

- **Step 1:** Trim the stems of soft herbs and place them in a glass of cold water, the way you would with fresh flowers.
- **Step 2:** You can keep these herbs at room temperature for about a week on a shelf in a cool area.
- **Step 3:** Alternatively, you can also place them in the refrigerator for a maximum of two weeks. Here, you want to loosely cover the leaves with a plastic bag to keep them fresh.

For hardy herbs such as thyme and rosemary, I recommend wrapping them loosely in a damp paper towel and storing them in a zip lock plastic bag in your refrigerator.

***Important Tips to Keep in Mind***

When you're harvesting your herbs for the first time, there are a few tips to keep in mind. I've listed them below for your convenience.

1. Properly wash and dry your herbs to ensure they remain as fresh as possible, for as long as possible.
2. To rinse your herbs, simply hold them under a mild stream of cold running water to get any soil off.
3. If you have a salad spinner, it's a good idea to use it to dry the excess water off your little herblings. You can also place them on a few dry paper towels to prevent wilting and to avoid potential mold and bacteria from setting in.
4. Ensure that your herbs are dry before storing them. Keep in mind that as with most other foods you want to keep dry, dampness can be a major enemy.

## PRESERVING THE BOUNTY: DRYING AND FREEZING YOUR HERBS

If you have started your herb garden with a few little herbs on the windowsill, then storage may not be your biggest concern. However, if you've jumped into your herb gardening dream with both feet and you've created a backyard or outdoor container paradise, you may need to learn some handy herb-preserving tips. Fortunately, I've been at both ends of this scenario and have learned some valuable tricks along the way. Before I share what I've learned, there are two facts I want you to know before you even plant your first seedling:

**Fact 1:** Drying and freezing are quite possibly the most effective methods to preserve your precious little herbs for effective long-term storage.

**Fact 2:** The types of drying and freezing methods that you choose will determine the flavor of your herbs. This will ultimately impact the recipes you want to use them in.

Being aware of these two facts will help you create the best storage method possible. After all, you wouldn't want to reach this point and watch your herbs wilt away on a shelf!

### Drying and Freezing Tips

That said, here are a few tips that I've either learned the hard way or seen other gardeners have success with. I urge you to stick to these tips to get the best out of your herb freezing and storage.

- **Small bunches:** An effective way to dry herbs is to tie them in small bunches and hang them upside down in a dry, warm, and dark place. Once your herbs are completely dry, strip the leaves from the stems and stalks and store them in airtight containers. It's a good idea to label the herbs with the date you've packed them. If you've opted to grow herbs that can be harvested more than once a season, it's a good idea to use the oldest herbs on your shelf first. That means, if you harvested in early April, and then again in mid-April, you should start by using the early April herbs first. As your herb supply starts filling your pantry shelf, it may be a good idea to invest in a few handy spice bottles—just be sure that they are airtight.

- **Freezing options:** Many gardeners—and even chefs—prefer the look and texture of fresh herbs in their dishes (usually salads and vegetarian dishes where you can still see the herb as well as taste it). In this instance, you can opt to freeze your herblings in water or olive oil in ice cube trays. That way, you can just pop the ice cube into your dish or pot without having it defrost. Many people prepare little ice cubes with all the necessary herbs and spices to reduce prep time on the day. If you have a big enough space in your freezer, you can also freeze the herb leaves flat on a baking sheet before eventually transferring them to a freezer bag. Once again, always opt for a zip lock bag to keep air and moisture out.

- **Drying herbs in the oven:** This is a method I don't recommend at all. While many people swear by it, my personal experience has been that you end up destroying the goodness in your herbs. There are many factors to consider such as cooling rack placement, air circulation, and temperature. It's much easier to roast your herbs in the process, rendering them utterly useless. Keep in mind that basic home dehydrators often have the same effect. If you're going to use a dehydrator, always opt for the lowest setting and keep an eye on them.

While drying and freezing is the best option for most herbs, keep in mind that some herbs such as basil, tarragon, mint, dill, and parsley lose a considerable amount of flavor when they're dried. These herbs are better frozen. The texture of frozen herbs is also softer and if not chopped too finely, will add a wonderful texture to your dish. Whether you freeze or dry your herbs comes down to your personal preference.

I would recommend making a simple dish with frozen herbs and then making the dish in the exact same way using dried herbs. Let your palate decide whether freezing or drying is best in your kitchen! It's also a great way to test which method provides you with the best-tasting herbs. I must point out that there isn't a hard-and-fast rule that applies to everyone. Factors such as humidity and general heat levels can affect drying conditions in your home.

With that in mind, it's time to take a look at how fresh herbs can significantly change the flavor of your food. Keep reading as I recommend a few ways to incorporate fresh herbs into your cooking!

# 7

# FROM GARDEN TO TABLE: UNLEASHING THE POWER OF YOUR HERBS

As for the garden of mint, the very smell of it alone recovers and refreshes our spirits, as the taste stirs up our appetite for meat.

— PLINY THE ELDER

I f you enjoy Italian pasta dishes or even Asian stir-fries, then you're no stranger to the alluring effect fresh herbs can have on your taste buds. Herbs such as basil, thyme, sage, marjoram, parsley, and oregano are the top herbs chosen for their delicious flavor profiles.

It's important to note that to enjoy your herbs to their fullest, it's essential to pair them with the right ingredients to create the perfect dish. With so many options at your fingertips, adding herbs to your different dishes can be a real treat. However, it can be quite daunting if you're not sure where to start. Fortunately, this chapter will give you a good starting point.

## UNDERSTANDING YOUR HERBS: FLAVOR PROFILES AND PAIRINGS

Understanding herb pairings can help you incorporate herbs more effectively, and this in turn will enhance not only the taste but also the aroma of your dish. Whether you're making a simple salad or a more complex meaty dish, herbs will only make it better. The best place to start is to know which pairings work well together. So, let's take a closer look at what pairings make great matches.

| Food | Top Pairing Herbs |
|:---:|:---:|
| **Rice** | Cumin, nutmeg, parsley, saffron, turmeric, chives, and the herbs that make up various curry mixes. |
| **Pork** | Basil, oregano, paprika, parsley, thyme, rosemary, cardamom, ginger, cloves, and marjoram. |
| **Lamb** | Dill, marjoram, mint, rosemary, cardamom, turmeric, dill, paprika, oregano and basil. |
| **Poultry** | Dill, sage, tarragon, thyme, marjoram, nutmeg, anise, bay leaf, parsley, and tarragon. |
| **Beef** | Dill, oregano, thyme, rosemary, marjoram, paprika, cayenne, parsley, ginger, and bay leaf. |
| **Fish** | Chives, ginger, oregano, tarragon, thyme, parsley, fennel, dill, basil, and thyme. |
| **Vegetables** | Carrots: Rosemary, thyme, parsley, and dill. Broccoli: Sage and nutmeg. Green beans: Marjoram and dill. Eggplant: Parsley and oregano. Cucumbers: Dill, basil, and parsley. |
| **Fruit** | Cinnamon, ginger, cloves, anise, and mint. |

Many herbs such as basil, marjoram, and parsley are extremely versatile and can be used in a wide variety of dishes. While it's true that certain dishes benefit from the addition of certain herbs, I always recommend experimenting with pairings to find the variation that suits your taste buds most. Experimenting with variations will help you create or improve your very own signature dish.

Once you start experimenting, be sure to make notes in your recipe journal so that you can replicate the options your family loves!

## COOKING WITH HERBS: TECHNIQUES AND TIPS

Adding herbs to increase or create a particular flavor is only the first step of the process. Keep in mind that the way and the time you add the herbs also make a huge difference in the overall flavor profile.

Here are a few top tips to keep in mind:

- **Adding early:** Hard herbs, such as thyme and rosemary, should be added early in the cooking process so that the flavor draws out of the herbs. A good example of this is cooking roast chicken. By adding rosemary at the beginning of the cooking process, you'll notice that the herb infuses with the meat, creating a deep, aromatic flavor.
- **Adding later:** Soft herbs such as cilantro and basil are usually added just before serving so that the flavor isn't cooked away in a long cooking process. Pasta sauce is a classic example of this. Adding basil a few minutes before serving piping hot tomato sauce will add a burst of fresh crispiness to whatever you're pouring the sauce over.

- **Knowing the flavor difference:** You may think that an herb tastes the same, no matter how you have it. But this isn't the case. By that, I mean that while herbs can be dried or fresh in your dish, the two forms aren't interchangeable. So, if your recipe calls for fresh parsley, keep in mind that adding the dried version won't provide you with the same flavor. It's important to note that dried herbs are stronger in flavor and should therefore be used in smaller quantities. You may have to adjust the amount you use to avoid overpowering your dish. This is especially the case with stronger herbs such as mint and ginger. As a rule of thumb, I usually use one-third of the amount of dried herbs that I would use as fresh. For instance, if my recipe calls for 1 tablespoon of fresh rosemary, I will use only 1 teaspoon of dried rosemary. For the most part, this will be a trial-and-error situation based on your personal preference.

## SIMPLE AND DELICIOUS HERB-BASED RECIPES

A quick online search will highlight just how many herb recipes make it easy for you to showcase the delightful flavors of your freshly grown herbs. For instance, give your regular roast chicken dish a rosemary garlic twist. Or alternatively, ditch the store-bought pesto sauce for your own basil pesto, created with fresh ingredients. The fresher, more robust flavor will have you making basil your new go-to herb!

Furthermore, herbs are not only excellent flavorings for meat dishes, pasta, and salads but also make a wonderful addition to desserts and drinks. Ever sprinkled freshly chopped mint over your chocolate ice cream? Try it—you won't be sorry! Looking for a way to spruce up your usual summer lemonade? A few sprigs of fresh mint are the secret ingredient to do just that.

A few other fun and tasty options to try include the following:

- **Lemon-basil potato salad:** Adding fresh lemon and basil to your next potato salad will take this old classic from drab to fab in an instant.
- **Strawberry-basil mojitos:** Tired of the same old summer cocktails? Surprise your guests with a new spin on the well-loved mojito. Simply replace the mint with fresh basil and include a few juicy strawberries.
- **Lime cilantro rice:** If there's one dish that your family may easily get bored with, it's most likely rice. Spruce up this dinnertime staple with some fresh cilantro and lime. This pairing combination will make for the most interesting dish on the table.

- **Marjoram mushrooms:** Looking for a fun new appetizer for your next dinner party? Add marjoram mushrooms to the shortlist.
- **Spaghetti with mushrooms, oregano, and garlic:** This wonderful pairing is one of the reasons that Italian pasta dishes are a firm favorite around the globe. The addition of oregano gives this simple dish a wonderful burst of flavor.
- **Indian lamb chops with a turmeric marinade:** Some herbs can also be used as a marinade. One such example is turmeric. In addition to using it in curries, this bright yellow herb is excellent as a marinade to use the next time you want to give your lamb chops a tasty twist.
- **Tarragon tuna salad:** It's very easy to get bored with salads if you're using the same ingredients and dressings all the time. One of the easiest ways to take the boredom out of your lunchtime salad is to add a robust herb such as tarragon. Add to tuna, chicken, or even beef strip salad. It's also a wonderful way to add a burst of color.
- **Mint feta dip:** Do you regularly serve snacks? Furthermore, do you like to serve a deliciously tangy dip for your carrot and celery sticks, sliced baguettes, or even toasted pita chips? Then this feta cheese and mint combination is a must-try.
- **Rosemary salmon and veggies:** The wonderful flavor that herbs add isn't limited to salads and meat. For added nutritional value and an exciting

flavor boost, add rosemary to your next plate of salmon and veggies.

- **Cinnamon basil ice cream**: Believe it or not, herbal ice creams are an actual thing. Aside from adding mint for that crispy fresh flavor, you can also consider adding an unusual herb called cinnamon basil. As the name implies, it's a combination of basil and cinnamon—in one plant —and is sometimes referred to as Mexican basil. Finding the herb in seed form may prove to be difficult as it's mostly grown via propagation. If you can get your hands on a cinnamon basil plant, it's a keeper!

- **Cheddar and chive mashed potatoes:** While mashed potatoes are a staple in just about every home, the dish can get boring very quickly. One of the best ways to spruce up a plate of mash is to add a combination of cheddar cheese and chives. Add some chopped, already-cooked sausage of your choice, too, and you'll have a dish even picky kids will love.

### A Few Tips for Cooking with Fresh Herbs

If you're going to be cooking with herbs for the first time, you may have a few questions about *how exactly* you add them to your various dishes. Consider these few simple tips to get you started:

1. **Be ready to experiment**: Robust herbs such as rosemary and thyme have a wonderful flavor profile. Don't be afraid to experiment with these herbs in your different meat and salad dishes. Also, don't be limited by the popular or traditional uses of herbs—use them to create your own dishes or spruce up dishes you've become bored with. Since herbs can be added in their raw form or cooked into dishes, your experimenting options are quite endless.

2. **Always use a sharp knife:** Herbs are versatile, and you can chop them finely or simply use rough chunks. Either way, you're going to want a sharp knife. Using a dull knife can cause the leaves to bruise, which in turn causes the flavor to seep out faster. This can affect the eventual flavor profile. If you're chopping straight after harvesting and just before freezing, the same rule of using a sharp knife applies. For meaty dishes, I always recommend chopping your herbs finely immediately before storing them in oil in your ice cube trays. A super sharp pair of kitchen scissors is also an excellent choice to simplify the process!

3. **Don't forget the sweets:** Herbs aren't just for meaty dishes, sauces, or salads. A few sprigs of flavorful herbs are an excellent way to add a pop of fresh color and a burst of flavor to an otherwise sweet treat. A few favorites to consider include basil leaves sprinkled over your peach ice cream,

lavender-infused lemon meringue pie, any of your favorite smoothies, and, of course, fresh mint chocolate chip ice cream pies. Encourage everyone to eat the herbs and not to scoop them off the ice cream. It's a great way for kids to get an extra vitamin boost. Be sure to chop them as finely as possible to make scooping them off the ice cream not quite so easy!

## HEALTH BENEFITS OF COOKING WITH FRESH HERBS

In addition to their culinary uses, fresh herbs are equally popular for their wide range of health benefits. For instance, turmeric is well-known for its anti-inflammatory properties while mint is commonly used for its digestive benefits. Additionally, rosemary is rich in antioxidants. With properties such as these, it's no wonder then that people opt to ditch pharmaceutical medications for healthier herb options.

Incorporating fresh herbs into your daily meal plans can easily contribute to your overall health and well-being without the risk of gut health side effects posed by some medications.

Adding herbs to your daily diet can be as simple as brewing a cup of mint or chamomile tea with your dinner to aid in digestion. Furthermore, certain herbs such as parsley and basil, are rich in vitamin C and vitamin D respectively. Adding herbs to your meals and drinks (smoothies and teas) is also a much easier way to get your family to take their daily vitamins!

Being aware of the various nutritional values offered by herbs is an excellent way to increase each meal's nutritional value. Keep reading as I take a more in-depth look at the health benefits offered by the most common herb choices!

# 8

# THE HEALING GARDEN: UNLEASHING THE POWER OF YOUR HERBS

*The famous herbalist Samuel Thompson used two herbs mainly, cayenne and lobelia. With those two herbs, it is estimated he helped 3.5 million people recover from their illnesses.*

— RICHARD M. SCHULZEX

For many people, the health benefits of herbs are nothing new. In fact, the healing properties of these little plants are even widely documented by the World Health Organization. As part of their 12-step healthy eating program, they recommend eating a nutritious diet based on a variety of plant-based foods which include beneficial herb leaves and flowers (World Health Organization, 2010).

The fact that herbs are not only tasty but add nutritional value to any meal or drink they're added to is another top reason to get started on your herb gardening journey sooner rather than later! Let's take a more in-depth look at the healing benefits of different herbs.

## UNLOCKING THE HEALING POWER OF HERBS

With busy work schedules and long commutes, it's often easier to resort to fast food for dinner. Furthermore, trying to cook nutritious meals can often be hampered by a lack of healthy ingredients. There can be many reasons for this—cost, seasonal availability, and overly processed ingredients are among the more prominent. With that said, growing your own herbs is one of the easier and more cost-effective ways to give all your meals a quick nutritional boost.

Incorporating a wider variety of fresh herbs into your meal planning will provide your family with nutrients such as vitamins A, C, and K. Minerals such as potassium, magnesium, and iron are also commonly found in many herbs. Knowing which herbs are the healthiest can become a top factor in helping you decide which ones you want to start your garden with. To help you, I've compiled a list of the top herbs and what their health benefits are.

1. **Oregano:** Excellent for its anti-inflammatory, antiviral, and antifungal properties, oregano can be added to your meals in fresh or dried forms and can also be infused with healthy oils such as olive, avocado, or peanut oil.

2. **Rosemary:** Rosemary is a very versatile herb that aids digestion, treats respiratory problems, fights bad breath, combats gastrointestinal conditions, and can also relieve stress. As a natural diuretic, it's also great to use in combination with blood pressure medication. It can be added to meaty dishes, pasta sauces, desserts, and even infused in tea.

3. **Turmeric:** One of the herbs with the most well-known reputation for anti-inflammatory benefits is without a doubt turmeric. In fact, you'll often find turmeric on the list of natural methods to combat everything from flu to anxiety. It's also excellent for regulating muscle soreness after exercise and even aiding kidney health. Including turmeric in your meals is as simple as adding a teaspoon or two to meat and poultry stews and

casseroles. Adding a teaspoon to your rice will give it a yellow color without altering the flavor. Keep in mind that turmeric powder is a golden yellow color, so don't be surprised by a change of color in your meaty dishes.

4. **Basil:** Regarded by many as the herb with the most health benefits, basil is another plant with a reputation for antibacterial and anti-inflammatory properties. With its powerful phytochemicals, basil is also known to kill many strains of unhealthy and harmful bacteria such as E. coli. It's also a super easy way to boost your general immunity. Basil can be added to everything from meat to salads, making it very easy to include in a healthy meal plan.

5. **Sage:** Many herbs are used to create teas, making it easier to take advantage of their health benefits. One such herb is sage. When drunk as tea, it can help lower blood sugar levels, remove fatty acids in the blood, and, in the process, improve insulin sensitivity. Swapping two of your daily sodas or caffeinated drinks for a fresh-infused sage tea will have you feeling more energetic in no time.

6. **Parsley:** Many people mistakenly regard parsley as a mere table garnish and in the process tend to overlook this versatile herb's actual nutritional value. So, yes, parsley is a lot more than just a dash of color. For one, it is packed with vitamin A, vitamin B, vitamin C, as well as vitamin K. High

iron properties, as well, improve blood clotting, and rich potassium levels regulate fluids in the body. Additionally, parsley also reduces water retention because of its excellent natural diuretic properties.

7. **Cilantro:** I must start by telling you that cilantro is not everyone's cup of tea. This is because many people say that cilantro tastes like soap! As a person who loves cilantro, I urge you to try it for yourself before believing the soap-tasting theories. With its antibacterial and antifungal properties, it's an effective barrier against salmonella and can easily remove toxic heavy metals from your body. It's also a well-known treatment against food poisoning, like listeria, and is commonly used to neutralize poison toxins.

8. **Mint:** Due to its delicious taste, mint is one of the more common herbs. However, it's not just popular for its crisp, fresh taste but also its health benefits. You may already know that it's excellent for reducing bad breath, but it's also more commonly associated with the relaxing effect its menthol compound has on the digestive tract.

9. **Lavender:** Another very beneficial herb that's a staple in many new and existing gardens is lavender. While lavender is not the most popular herb to add to food, it's a firm favorite for tea. Brewed as a fresh, hot tea, it can treat skin blemishes, improve sleep, reduce blood pressure,

lessen symptoms associated with menstruation or menopause, and even promote hair growth. When used as an essential oil, it can also be used as a migraine headache relief. Another benefit of having lavender in pots around the house is that it's a natural repellent to those pesky bugs you don't want in your home such as flies, ants, and even mosquitos.

### Growing Organically Makes All the Difference

To get store-bought benefits out of your herbs, it's important to note that growing them organically is the way to go. As I've mentioned previously, organic herb gardening removes the use and exposure to harmful chemicals. So, to enjoy herbs for their full benefits, I always recommend opting for organic gardening practices.

A little-known fact is that store-bought herbs that are randomly tested are often found to have traces of pesticide residues which erase many of their health properties.

## COOKING FOR HEALTH: USING HERBS IN YOUR MEALS

Healthy meal prep is often regarded as time-consuming and complicated. However, making a few healthy food choices and incorporating your organically grown herbs will make all the difference, and what's more, it's easier than you think!

Even a small sprinkle with every meal can provide considerable health benefits. In addition to their individual properties, most herbs share a common property, which is to reduce inflammation. Here are a few more ways to incorporate herbs into your meals:

- **Cooking:** Use fresh herbs, such as parsley and basil, as a garnish, and enjoy the fresh and vibrant taste and color in cooked meals as well as mixed into your salad.
- **Use for breakfast or lunchtime smoothies and tea:** If you enjoy a breakfast or lunchtime smoothie, why not give it an extra nutritional boost? Adding some finely chopped herbs is an excellent addition to just about any smoothie, and you can easily infuse your own flavor combinations. Furthermore, warm or iced herbal teas are a huge plus due to their health benefits and amazing flavor profile. Common herbal teas are chamomile, lavender, mint, and sage—all commonly used for their calming effects.
- **Add to oils:** Many recipes, especially those made with oils or butter, offer a wonderful opportunity for adding your herbs. If you're a bit hesitant about overcooking your herbs at first, opt to heat them with your cooking oil or unsalted butter. This will not only draw out but also extend the flavor of your herbs. Doing this is great when you're frying onions or garlic before adding the

remaining ingredients. If you're mixing your herbs with salad oils, ensure that your oil of choice is at room temperature.

## PRESERVING THE GOODNESS: STORING HERBS FOR HEALTH

To ensure that you get the maximum benefits from your herbs, it's important to store them correctly. As I've already mentioned in Chapter 7, there are a few different ways to store your herbs after harvesting. In addition to those guidelines, always keep the following in mind:

- Always keep dry herbs in a cool, dry place.
- Containers, whether glass or plastic, should be airtight. If you're using plastic bags, opt for zip lock options.
- Regularly check your herbs to ensure that they are still dry and fresh.
- Discard any that show signs of mold, decay, or bacteria growth. Keep in mind that adding any moldy herbs to your cooking or salads will cause illness, respiratory problems, or even allergic reactions. I really want to stress that you can't merely wash mold off—the herbs should just be thrown away or put into your compost pile.

## GROWING A HEALTHIER FUTURE: THE IMPACT OF HERB GARDENING ON HEALTH

Growing your own herbs is about so much more than contributing to a healthier plate of food. The act of gardening has its own benefits for your overall health. These health benefits range from increasing your physical exercise to improving your mental well-being. Let's take a more detailed look at a few of the top ways that creating your herb garden dream will benefit your general well-being:

1. **It acts as a form of exercise:** While gardening may not be as intensive as a daily spinning class, the good news is that as a moderate-intensity level activity, setting up and taking care of your herb garden can contribute to you staying active and healthy. This is especially the case if you're planning to create an outdoor garden or even set up a container garden in your courtyard. Remember that even the mildest form of exercise is great for improving blood circulation and moving your muscles. Since you can place your herb pots, containers, or raised beds at a level that you can reach, you don't have to bend down to enjoy an herb garden.

2. **It boosts your mood:** A recent study from the Journal of Health Psychology has found that even the simplest forms of gardening can reduce stress

and also function as a great mood booster. Spending time gardening has been known to lower anxiety levels, ease feelings of depression, and improve overall mood.

3. **It promotes healthier eating habits:** Most people who grow herbs do so for the purpose of eating them. Only a small fraction of herbs, such as mint and lavender, are grown to deter household pests or to be used in bath and relaxation products. That said, growing herbs such as parsley, sage, and rosemary can provide you with access to fresh, organic herbs that increase the likelihood of you using them in your meals. Many gardeners who start out with herbs often begin including vegetables in their gardens to increase their organic crop. Opting to eat organic herbs and veggies can in turn improve heart and cholesterol health.

4. **It creates feelings of connection:** There's a reason why a pastime as old as gardening is still as popular as ever, even in a busy digital world. Not only does it provide you with healthy food options, but it's also an excellent way to connect with other people. I recommend joining a local community herb garden group. That way, you'll get to learn and share tips and hacks that will make your gardening process so much easier and fun. Furthermore, it's a great way to share herbs and veggies as well as get your hands on some

quality heirloom herbs and veggies that you can grow from cuttings!

Setting up your own herb garden is an excellent way to combat food shortages, increase your organic food consumption, and at the same time boost your vitamin and mineral intake. Additionally, since herbs are so easy to grow, just about anyone at any age and health status can do it.

One of the easiest ways to get some strong herbs in your garden is by propagating cuttings. These can be from your own first harvest or from other people's successful plants. Curious to learn how to do that? Read on to see how easy it is!

# 9

# PLANT PARENTHOOD: GROWING NEW HERBS FROM CUTTINGS

*I like to encourage people interested in gardening or planting to begin with a simple herb garden. Even if you live in a small apartment, you can have some herb pots.*

— ANNA GETTY

There are a few ways to get the actual herbs you want to grow. You can opt to buy seed packets or buy small herblings from your local nursery. However, one of the more effective ways to get your hands on a healthy herb is by propagation. It has also become my favorite way of collecting new herbs for my garden. What exactly is propagation and what is the best way to do it? Let's find out.

## UNDERSTANDING PROPAGATION

Essentially, propagation is the process of growing new herbs from existing plants. This can be done by using pieces of the herb (referred to as cuttings), bulbs, seeds from a live plant, and in some cases other plant parts such as leaves or stalks. Simply put, you're growing a new plant from a piece of an existing one.

A 2015 study published by the Journal of Applied Research on Medicinal and Aromatic Plants highlights that propagation using cuttings is the most reliable method to grow multiple plants, particularly herbs.

Furthermore, the New York Botanical Garden has listed propagation as the most sustainable gardening practice as it reduces the need to buy new plants. It's also a very effective way to create sustainable large-scale community gardening as you're essentially using healthy, heirloom plants to create bigger gardens. This is a common practice where herb and vegetable gardens are created as part of organic food projects.

## THE SCIENCE BEHIND SUCCESSFUL PROPAGATION

Understanding how propagation works is not complicated. In fact, it all comes down to the herb's ability to produce several new cells and, in the process, grow a new and healthy root system. This process is commonly referred to as rooting.

The reason propagation is so successful has to do with using parts from a healthy and vigorous parent plant that already has the necessary nutrients and cells to create a new shoot. Of course, you will need to ensure that you are propagating in the right conditions to be successful.

It's also important to keep in mind that different herbs have varying propagation timelines and success rates. A good example of this is mint and rosemary. Mint can be propagated with very little hassle while rosemary, on the other hand, requires more attention and effort.

## THE ART OF TAKING CUTTINGS

Before you start butchering your neighbor's mint shrub, it's important to note that there is some skill required to take successful cuttings. To help you with this, simply follow the easy steps listed below.

1. **Look for a healthy parent plant:** You're going to need a healthy parent plant that is not only robust but also disease and fungus-free. Ideally, you should only consider propagating from a plant that has grown a strong root system. This means it should be at least one full season old and fully grown.

2. **Select a strong green stem:** Select a strong, green stem that you're going to use as your first cutting. You'll need to use your sharp kitchen or pruning scissors to snip just below a leaf node (this is the area where the leaves come out of the stem). Cut a piece that's about three to four inches long. For softwood herbs such as oregano and mint, use newly grown stems. Hardwood herbs such as lavender and rosemary will do better growing from mature, woody stems.

3. **Remove any lower leaves:** Since you're going to put the cutting in a glass of water, you'll want to remove all the lower leaves. Keeping the leaves on, under the water, will lead to bacteria and mold growth. Opt for a clear glass so that the cutting can absorb maximum light.

4. **Choose a sunny windowsill:** Place the glass on a sunny windowsill, facing south. You will need to change the water every few days to reduce the likelihood of bacteria growth as well as to encourage growth. This process will require some patience as it can take anywhere from four to six

weeks to see new roots sprouting out of the bottom of your cutting. Since some herbs can root slower than others, it may take as long as eight weeks.

5. **Plant when roots appear:** When your little cutting starts rooting, your cutting will be ready for planting. You'll do this by filling a pot or container loosely with rocks, twigs, and leaves for drainage and then adding some compost and soil. Poke a hole into the middle of the pot and lower the cutting into the hole. Be sure to make a hole big enough to comfortably fit the roots that have started growing. Press the compost and soil down to secure the plant. Do the same process for backyard planting, minus the pot, of course!

6. **Water your new herb:** Water the new herb, but don't overwater it. Perform regular checks to ensure that there are no pests or diseases present.

## ENCOURAGING ROOT GROWTH

Often, the steps highlighted above can get stuck at the root phase as some herbs take longer than others. To encourage root growth, consider the following tips:

1. **Rooting hormones:** Consider using a rooting hormone to increase the chances of success. Rooting hormones are available from your local nursery or garden center, usually in powder form.

You can also make your own rooting hormone by dipping your cutting into some raw honey or aloe vera gel. Alternatively, you can place the cutting in coconut water to provide additional nutrients.

2. **Creating a greenhouse effect:** For some cuttings, placing them on a sunny windowsill isn't enough to get them sprouting. In these cases, you may have to create a mini greenhouse effect. Do this by placing a small, clear plastic bag over the cutting. Ensure that the bag covers the whole cutting but still has some airflow. Two small holes in the bag will ensure this. Doing this will create a warm, humid environment.

## TRANSPLANTING AND AFTERCARE

Whether you're propagating from seeds or from a cutting, it's important to let your new herbling develop a strong rooting system before you transplant it to its permanent spot. I usually wait until the new herb has a very robust network of young roots before transplanting. This is to avoid the initial shock the plant experiences when it's suddenly placed in a new environment.

It's also not uncommon for a root to get damaged when you're transplanting it. This means that if your little herb only has a single root, and that gets damaged, the herb may not survive. That's why I recommend waiting till there are a few strong and firm roots before relocating. If you're worried about nutrients, simply put a little honey or coconut water into the glass with every water change.

Another tip I'd like to share involves acclimatizing the new plant before placing it in your outdoor garden. This is so that the herb becomes familiar with its new environment so that it can slowly get used to it. Here's how you do that:

- **Day 1:** Once roots appear, take the makeshift plastic greenhouse off of the glass and let it sit on a windowsill with the window open. Ideally, you want a windowsill where there's a light breeze.
- **Day 2–4:** Take the glass outside in the early morning for about an hour. Place it in a shady spot (on a table or chair) so that the herb can start getting used to the wind and natural light without being scorched by direct sunlight. Do this for about three days at different times of the day.
- **Day 5:** On the fourth day, leave the plant outside for two hours. On the fifth day, try leaving it out for three to four hours.
- **Day 6:** After a week, leave the plant outside for the whole day, and start leaving it out till the early evening.
- **Day 7:** If your little herb doesn't seem to be wilting, then this means it's acclimatizing and may soon be ready for transplanting into its container or backyard spot.

I must admit, many of my herbs acclimatize a lot sooner than seven days, while a few have required some more coaxing. It really depends on the humidity, amount of direct sunlight, and, of course, the type of herb. The average time is anywhere between seven to ten days.

## TROUBLESHOOTING PROPAGATION PROBLEMS

Once you've done it a few times, the propagation process is quite straightforward. However, beginner gardeners may encounter a few common problems that make it seem like a complex process. Some of the more common issues are listed below.

1. **Failure to root:** While generally an effective process, some cuttings simply don't root. Failure to root is normally a sign that the conditions weren't right, or the cutting was taken at the wrong time of the season. To avoid this, always familiarize yourself with the best time in the season to take a specific cutting. It's also a good idea to take several cuttings if possible, to increase your chances of a successful propagation.

2. **Signs of disease on the stem of the cutting:** If the stalk or stem that you've taken as your cutting shows signs of disease, it may mean that you haven't changed the water in the glass often enough. Be sure to change the water at least every second day and remember to add more rooting

hormones or honey to boost nutrient intake.
Check the stem and remaining top leaves for
disease. If the cutting has a confirmed disease, you
will have to discard it as there's no root system in
place yet to create new, healthy cells.

3. **The stem seems to be wilting:** This may be a
   clear indication that the cutting isn't receiving
   enough sunlight. Be sure to rotate it on the
   windowsill, as you would a rooted herb in a pot.
   Remember to add a little makeshift greenhouse
   bag to create a humid growing environment.

There are many benefits to plant propagation. By using a
cutting from an established herb, you're ensuring that you
are replicating the quality of the parent plant. It's also
considerably easier than trying to get herbs to grow from
a seed packet, which is sometimes difficult. Fortunately,
creating new herbs from cuttings is easy—all you have to
do is follow my guidelines.

By getting cuttings from your social circle, you'll be able
to have a thriving herb garden in no time. With that in
mind, I believe it's also important to take a look at a few of
the more unusual herbs to consider adding to your garden
once you've established a basic garden. Read on for a look
at the more unusual herblings seasoned gardeners include
in their herb gardens!

# 10

# BEYOND THE BASICS: DISCOVERING UNUSUAL HERBS FOR YOUR GARDEN

*Gardening is cheaper than therapy - and you get tomatoes. –*

— ANONYMOUS

When you start chatting about herb gardening, there are a few herbs that likely always come to mind. Parsley, sage, thyme, rosemary, mint, and lavender are among the top favorites that make it to just about every herb garden. This is mostly because they're easy to grow and perhaps more importantly, they're super tasty when added to various dishes.

However, there are a bunch of lesser-known herbs that feature their own unique and flavorsome qualities in your dishes. Furthermore, adding a few of these not-so-common herblings to your new garden will create wonderful garden diversity. Let's explore a few of these lesser-known herb varieties.

## UNEARTHING THE UNCOMMON: VENTURING INTO LESSER-KNOWN HERBS

When you embark on your herb gardening journey, there's no hard-and-fast rule that you should only grow the easy, more common options. While it's true that they're excellent to start with, there's no reason why you can't expand your garden once it's established. Here are a few of my favorite lesser-known herbs worth considering:

1. **Lovage:** More commonly known as an old-world herb, lovage boasts a celery-like flavor and looks similar to its more well-known cousin. With its fresh taste, it's a great addition to tuna or chicken

salad and even fresh tomato salsa. In some parts of the world, lovage is referred to as sea parsley and is a must-add to pork and poultry dishes as well as stews and soups.

2. **Lemon balm:** As a member of the mint family, lemon balm is another old-world herb that was more commonly used in the medieval ages to treat stress and anxiety. It's also a natural way to treat the pain and irritation associated with indigestion which includes bloating and gas. You can brew your lemon balm into a tea, or even throw some fresh leaves into your water bottle. Some people also choose to make a balm out of it to treat cold sores.

3. **Borage:** This is another herb well known for its healing properties. Many people grow borage to use as a treatment for kidney ailments, as a diuretic, and even as a sedative. The leaves are dried to be used as tea while the seeds are pressed to create borage oil, often used as an herbal supplement. If you love the taste of cucumber, then this herb is a must-have in your garden.

4. **Fenugreek:** Despite being on the unusual herb list, fenugreek is often found in existing herb gardens. This is because its robust flavor is excellent for slow-cooked dishes. This is especially the case when you want to add a boost of flavor to gamey meats such as lamb and goat. It's also an excellent medicinal herb and is traditionally used

as part of treatments for obesity, diabetes, and painful menstruation. As a supplement, it is also used for treating various heart health issues such as high blood pressure and cholesterol.

5. **Anise:** For the most part, anise is more commonly used for its medicinal properties. It has been known to work for upset stomachs, as a diuretic, and even as an appetite stimulant. With its unusual flavor profile, it is a common addition to desserts.

6. **Chervil:** The best way to describe the flavor of chervil is to say that it is a combination of tarragon and parsley. It also has a faint licorice profile, making it a tasty addition as a dessert garnish. Its medicinal properties include being useful for the treatment of skin conditions, gout, and even digestion problems. While it may look like parsley, an easy way to tell them is apart is by their feathery leaves, which are sometimes bigger than those of their distant relative.

7. **Feverfew:** Instantly recognized as a member of the daisy family, feverfew boasts lovely little white and yellow flowers. It is typically used in tea to treat stomachaches, toothaches, migraine headaches, and even rheumatoid arthritis. If the name sounds a little unusual, you may recognize it from one of its other names, bachelor's button or even wild chamomile.

8. **Stevia:** Essentially, stevia is a sugar substitute, and its leaves are considerably sweeter than regular, processed table sugar. With no carbohydrates, artificial additives, or calories, it's a common replacement for sugar. Commonly known to reduce blood pressure and increase urine output, it's important to note that its taste isn't everyone's cup of tea. Some people find it bitter (compared to regular sugar), while others enjoy the crisp menthol taste.

9. **Horehound:** As another mint cousin, horehound is more commonly known as an ingredient in cough drops. With a flavor that has been described as a mix of root beer and menthol, it's easy to see why its medicinal properties are so popular. Used as a tea, horehound can be used to treat ailments such as loss of appetite, diarrhea, bloating, and even gas.

10. **Cinnamon basil:** As a distant cousin of the traditional basil herb, cinnamon basil, also sometimes called Mexican basil, boasts the benefits of basil combined with those of cinnamon. Its unique and mild cinnamon combination makes it a firm favorite in both Thai and Italian cuisines. Additionally, infusing it as a tea releases its highly beneficial health benefits which include treating headaches, kidney problems, diarrhea, constipation, and even warts.

## PLANTING AND CARING FOR UNUSUAL HERBS

As with the more common herbs, the unusual options also have their own set of growing requirements. A few tips to consider when you're considering planting a few of the unusual herbs are listed below.

1. **Lovage:** This delightful herb prefers part shade and well-draining soil. Since this herb grows quite tall, you will need to leave adequate space.
2. **Lemon balm:** As one of the herbs that's prone to bouts of powdery mildew, lemon balm should always be planted where it can get a lot of air circulation. If you're planting it on a windowsill, opt for a window that you can keep open regularly.
3. **Borage:** For the most part, borage is easy to grow, but you may need to keep an eye out for powdery mildew. Treat with mild soapy water and be sure to remove any plants that are severely affected. This is especially necessary if they are close to your other herbs. Remember to sterilize the tools you're using on this plant before using them on another plant.
4. **Fenugreek:** As with most herbs, fenugreek loves full sun and a lot of water. This is particularly important in dry spells or hot climates. You may want to add drip irrigation to your fenugreek herbs to ensure the soil remains moist.

5. **Anise:** Always plant your anise seedlings in early spring in a sunny area. These little herbs grow to be three inches tall and prefer a light, well-drained, moderately rich, sandy loam.

6. **Chervil:** This unusual herb enjoys partial shade and damp soil. Since they're a firm favorite of slugs and snails, it's important to watch out for these pests.

7. **Feverfew:** For your feverfew, opt for moist but never wet or totally dry soil. As part of the chamomile family, growing requirements will be the same.

8. **Stevia:** Commonly known as a sun-loving plant, your stevia herb will want maximum sun and well-drained soil. You may need to feed it regularly with water-soluble plant food to ensure it produces the nutrients to promote healthy leaf production.

9. **Horehound:** As a hardy perennial related to mint, horehound prefers full sun combined with well-drained soil. Since seeds are slow to germinate, I recommend you sow your horehound seeds shallow enough to encourage optimum emergence. Since this medicinal herb grows to anywhere between 9 and 17 inches tall and branches out, it will need quite a bit of space in your garden. If you're planting it in a container pot, be sure to opt for a large pot.

10. **Cinnamon basil:** Just like its more famous cousin, the cinnamon basil variant is relatively easy to grow. It requires six to eight hours of strong sunlight per day and germination usually takes between 5 to 14 days. As one of the taller herb species, cinnamon basil grows to about 20 inches and needs space around it to flourish.

## COOKING WITH LESSER-KNOWN HERBS

If you're considering a few of these lesser-known herbs, you may be wondering how you're going to incorporate them into your cooking. Here are a few ways to get the best flavor profile from these uncommon options.

1. **Lovage:** For a celery-like flavor, chop lovage and add it to soups and stews.
2. **Lemon balm:** Make a soothing tea with lemon balm leaves. Add a touch of honey for extra flavor and nutritional value.
3. **Borage:** Since borage boasts a crisp taste similar to cucumber, it's a good idea to add it to salads. You can also use it as a garnish on desserts but chop it up first.
4. **Fenugreek:** These leaves add an extra boost of flavor to both hot and mild curry dishes.
5. **Anise:** If you enjoy the taste of licorice in your baked goods, then anise should definitely have a

space in your garden. It also adds an unusual but tasty flavor profile to salads.

6. **Chervil:** Despite a faint flavor similar to licorice or anise, chervil is often used to add a pop of flavor to omelets. Since it's part of the parsley family, it can also be used as a garnish substitute.

7. **Feverfew:** If you're looking to grow a medicinal herb garden, adding feverfew is a must. Commonly used to treat migraines, feverfew leaves can also be used to treat menstrual pain and insect bites.

8. **Stevia:** You can use stevia the way you would use sugar. That means you can add it to tea and coffee. As a natural sweetener, it makes a great alternative to honey and maple syrup.

9. **Horehound:** This is a must-have herb for anyone who enjoys making their own candies. As part of the mint family, it has a crisp and refreshing taste.

10. **Cinnamon basil:** With its unique, warm flavor combination, cinnamon basil is excellent as a garnish for both salads and desserts. You can also blend it into pesto, infuse it into oils and teas, or simply chop it up into stews, soups, and stir-fry dishes.

When trying out a new herb, always start with small quantities to see if you like the flavor combination. Some pairings will be better than others, but you won't know which ones you'll love until you start experimenting!

### EXPANDING YOUR HERBAL KNOWLEDGE

Part of creating a successful herb garden involves gathering as much knowledge as you can about the plants you're going to grow and harvest. Learning about herbs, their growth patterns, and their various applications will make you a better gardener and give your current cooking methods a secret edge.

A few top ways to improve your knowledge about regular and lesser-known herbs are listed below.

1. **Local gardening clubs:** Check out local gardening clubs in your area. Look for the ones that are specifically geared at herb gardening for beginners.
2. **Online platforms:** Join online forums and Facebook groups where you can ask questions and learn tips from experienced herb gardeners. Again, opting for beginner-specific groups will make it easier for you to ask the questions commonly asked by newbie gardeners.
3. **Experimenting with different plant types:** Experiment with growing and cooking techniques to find the options that you enjoy. Don't be afraid to discard the herbs you don't favor and replace them with other options. Rather, use your energy and resources to nurture herbs that you find

functional both in your cooking and for your medicinal purposes.

Now that you know a little more about both the regular and the unusual herbs out there, it's going to be much easier to find the best selection for your new garden. Once you have an idea of the types of herblings you're going to start with, it's important to focus on the climate, weather conditions, and easy ways to adapt your herb care to each season.

This involves changing your watering techniques as well as safeguarding your herbs against extreme weather conditions to ensure you have a thriving garden all year round! As with everything so far, it's much easier than you think! Let's dive in and see what it entails.

# 11

# SEASONS OF GROWTH: ADAPTING YOUR HERB GARDEN TO THE CHANGING CLIMATE

*Herbs are the thread that weaves together the tapestry of flavors in every recipe.*

— UNKNOWN

Whether you're planning to grow an indoor, outdoor, container, or even vertical herb garden, there's one crucial aspect that you need to factor into your planning—and that is understanding how the changing seasons impact your herb growth. Keep in mind that although windowsill gardens may not be directly in the wind and the cold, the amount and strength of sunlight affect their ability to survive from one season to the next.

That said, this chapter looks at how to apply specific care techniques to ensure that your little herblings not only thrive in but survive the different seasons.

## THE IMPACT OF SEASONS ON HERB GROWTH

Setting up an herb garden is a lot of work, especially in the beginning when you're adapting the soil and watering techniques to create the perfect environment. Surely this isn't something you want to do from scratch every year just to secure one season of herbs, is it?

Furthermore, the goal should always be to create a herb garden that grows stronger with each season as the roots become more established. Remember that a more established root system makes for a healthier plant that's more likely to produce top-quality herbs. And, since you're not only cooking in the summer, I think it's safe to say you're going to need your precious little herblings to survive the winter, snow, rain, hot sun, and any other harsh weather you may experience in your area!

Harsh weather such as severe storms can have a damaging effect on your little herbs if they aren't protected. Being waterlogged for days can have an adverse effect on your root system and a lack of sun will see your herbs wilting. It's a good idea to include herbs such as basil, chives, parsley, and rosemary that can survive the cooler months when there's less sun. That means you'll want to plant a varied mix of annual and perennial herbs to maintain a healthy garden throughout the year. Doing this will ensure that you have a wide range of herbs to enjoy in your winter stews, soups, and curries as well as your summer salads.

## ADAPTING HERB CARE TO EACH SEASON

To understand how each season impacts your herb care, let's take a closer look at some of the ways you should adapt your gardening techniques to ensure a thriving garden all year round.

### Spring

For most herbs, spring is the best time to plant—as early as possible in the season, too. Herbs that are started in the early spring have ample time to create an established root system before they are bolted by summer heat, rain, and, of course, the cold winter elements.

A few reminders to ensure that your herbs get off to a good start include the following:

- **Soil:** Ensure that you opt for a high-quality potting mix for windowsill, container, and vertical pots.
- **Water:** Practice the watering guidelines highlighted throughout this guide to give yourself the best chance of mastering the difference between over and underwatering.
- **Mulch and compost**: Add mulch and compost at the recommended times to ensure that you create a nutrient-rich foundation for your delicate herblings.
- **Sunlight:** The right amount of light is important to get your roots growing and your herbs sprouting. Don't forget to consider growing lights if you're struggling with your indoor plants.

### Summer

The summer months are the times when your herbs will be exposed to the most heat. If they have already started growing and extending their roots, they will stand a better chance of survival. It's also important to have established a tried and tested watering technique by the time summer rolls around.

Here are your summer tips to keep in mind:

- **The right time:** Most herbs need watering once the soil is dry to the touch. Always water in the early morning to avoid the bulk of the water being absorbed by the sun. Remember that water can scorch little herbs if done during midday when the water is cold, and the plants are hot.
- **Moving around:** Be sure to move your container and windowsill pots around to make sure they receive morning sunlight. If they're receiving more than eight hours of bright sunlight, it's a good idea to move them around for them to get some shade.

### Autumn

By Autumn your spring-planted annual herbs should be ready for harvesting. This is also the time of the year when you start preparing your perennial herbs for winter.

This is what you need to do in autumn:

- **Harvesting:** This is the time to harvest any remaining herbs that you may not already have harvested in the summer. This will especially be the case with herbs that were harvested early in summer and are now ready to be harvested again. Use the harvesting and storing guidelines discussed in Chapter 8 to ensure that you have fresh herbs to add to those winter stews, soups, casseroles, and curries.

- **Insulation:** For your outdoor gardens, autumn is the time when you start cutting back your perennial herbs and adding a thick layer of mulch under and around the whole garden. Doing this will provide an extra layer between the ground and the winter frost that could harm your herb's roots. Wood chips and grass cuttings make for good mulching options.

- **Moving container pots:** If you live in an area that can get very cold, and your container pots aren't too heavy to move, it's a good idea to move them out of the courtyard or space where they're going to be battered by snow. Moving them onto the deck or porch is a good idea. That way, your home will offer some shelter from the wind. You can also move them under a carport where they're still exposed to some sun.

- **Removing the annuals:** Annuals such as coriander, basil, and summer savory are usually the first of your herbs to die as they tend to feel the frost first. To me, it's a good indicator that winter has arrived. In this case, you should remove the wilted plants by pulling them out by the roots. There's no sense in soil nutrients being wasted trying to revive them! Chuck these plants in the compost so that they can be ready to be reused in the garden in the spring. Use your garden fork to loosen the soil and then place a layer of mulch over the area to protect the soil nutrients from any harsh weather.

### Winter

I'm sure I don't have to tell you this, but winter can be brutal in some parts of the US. Winter care for your herbs involves creating adequate protection for your outdoor plants as they bear the brunt of freezing temperatures. Indoor herbs will also require a certain amount of care to ensure they remain strong.

Winter herb care tips include the following:

- **Wrapping pots:** An old trick that experienced raised bed gardeners often do is wrap outdoor pots, raised beds, and containers in thick pieces of burlap. This is a great idea if you can't or don't want to move your pots around. The burlap provides the soil with additional heat, and in the process keeps the roots from freezing to death. If you're not moving the container pots, be sure to add mulch on top of the soil when you put the burlap on. If you don't have access to burlap, frost blankets, old indoor blankets or even bubble wrap will work just as well. Be sure to secure the cloth to the pot by tying a string around it at the top and bottom.

- **Creating more light:** Indoor plants may be sheltered from snow and wind, but they are also subject to less light and humidity in the winter. Move your windowsill pots to a south-facing windowsill if possible. Alternatively, invest in a grow light to help your herbs during those gloomy days when there's little to no sun.

## PREPARING YOUR HERB GARDEN FOR EXTREME WEATHER

You don't have to be an experienced gardener to know that extreme weather conditions such as heat waves, snow and rainstorms, and severe bouts of frost can seriously damage your herb plants. Fortunately, you don't have to stand on the porch and watch your poor little herbs being battered by the weather—there are a few things you can do to minimize the damage.

Some tips for keeping your herbs safe during those extreme weather moments include the following:

- **Use row covers:** Consider investing in row covers or plant blankets for your outdoor garden. Floating row covers, as they're also called, are little tents made of spun-bonded polyester or polypropylene material. They act as a windbreak by keeping extreme wind and rain from damaging your plants. Additionally, they retain heat, water, and air, and your plants can still see the sun. Unlike shade cloth, you won't need to create extra supports to hold the little tents up. For areas where extreme weather conditions are common, you can opt to put two layers of row covers over your herbs, but bear in mind that anything more than two layers will start reducing the amount of light that comes through.

- **Lift your containers:** If the area you're living in is prone to severe rainstorms in the winter, I recommend removing the container trays from underneath the pots to avoid the plants becoming waterlogged. You can also place the containers on bricks to minimize the amount of water that reaches the roots from the bottom. In these instances, you'll want to bulk up on the mulch. You may even have to add an additional layer on top of the one you added in the autumn. Straw, sawdust, pine needles, and pebbles are excellent for slowing down the excess water from streaming straight into the roots.

- **Keep watering:** Don't rely on the rain to keep your perennial herbs growing unless it rains every day. Be sure to check your plants for dry soil and give them just enough water to keep the ground moist. Since there's no harsh sunlight, you won't have to do this as often in the winter as you do in the summer.

- **See to some post-storm care:** If your garden gets battered by a severe storm, you will need to give your herbs some extra care to ensure they don't wilt due to storm stress. Do this by removing the damaged leaves, stems, and stalks as soon as possible. This prevents the broken pieces from generating mold, bacteria, and eventually disease. Removing the damaged parts also helps the plants focus their remaining energy and nutrients on new growth rather than trying to rehabilitate the injured pieces. Be sure to provide extra water and nutrients to the damaged plants to help them recover.

- **Dig holes in the garden:** If your backyard is usually drenched with seasonal rains, it may be a good idea to dig drainage holes around your herb garden. This will help to limit the amount of water that pools up on your herbs. If you have your herbs planted in rows, consider digging small holes in the spaces between the rows.

## EMBRACING SEASONALITY IN YOUR HERB GARDEN

The phrase "seasonality in your herb garden" refers to the concept of providing the care necessary to enjoy a wide variety of fresh herbs throughout the year. Achieving this is done by planting a healthy mixture of annual and perennial herbs, harvesting them, and then providing the care needed to get them through the cooler months.

Creating the most optimal growing conditions for your seasonal herbs is the best way to ensure that you can enjoy their robust flavor profiles throughout the year. Furthermore, seasonal gardening aligns perfectly with the sustainable living principles that may have driven you to create your own garden in the first place.

Not only does seasonal gardening reduce your reliance on store-bought herbs, but it also allows you to contribute and support your community's local biodiversity and ecologically sound farming practices.

The next chapter looks at those dreaded gardening hurdles that all gardeners have experienced, but don't really want to talk about! Knowing what can go wrong with your little herblings gives you the perfect opportunity to rescue them before it's too late. Keep reading for a few tips on combating the most common herb-growing challenges!

# 12

# OVERCOMING GARDEN HURDLES: ADDRESSING COMMON HERB GARDENING ISSUES

*There are no gardening mistakes, only experiments.*

— JANET KILBURN PHILIPS

Herb gardening is a wonderful hobby and an enriching way to improve the flavor and nutritional value of your food. Additionally, my gardening adventures are proof that growing herbs is something anyone can do with just the most basic resources. With that said, it's time for me to announce that it's not all smooth sailing!

I've mentioned this before, but I will say it again because it's important to keep in mind: *Every gardener, no matter how experienced, will at some point encounter a problem or two.* From slow growth to dull tastes, knowing how to troubleshoot these issues can save your plants, keep your garden thriving, and keep your spirits up! I've compiled a few of the more common issues you may potentially encounter and what you can do about them.

## SEEDS NOT GROWING: A MAJOR LETDOWN

Many first-time gardeners rush out and buy a ton of seed packets with the intention of turning their backyard into an herb oasis. While there's nobility in the concept, it doesn't always pan out that way. One of my earliest gardening disasters was investing more money than I should have into seed packets that never grew! Imagine my disappointment!

**The cause:** In many instances, herbs don't always grow from seed. This can be due to many factors in your environment.

**The solution:** I always tell first-time gardeners to invest in herb starter kits for the first round of herbs. This means that you'll be able to grow your herbs from a healthy foundation, reducing the risk of seeds not sprouting at all. Additionally, ask people in your social circle for cuttings from some of their heirloom herbs. That way, you'll be sure that the root system is established, making it easier to grow.

However, if you have no alternative but to use seed packets, consider germinating the seeds indoors until they are a few inches high before replanting them in your outdoor garden or courtyard containers. Always follow the exact instructions listed on the seed packet to give your herb the best possible chance. Also, opt for the herbs that are the easiest to grow, to test your soil and improve your gardening skills. Avoid planting complex herbs that require intricate, extensive care until you have mastered your watering, pruning, and harvesting skills.

## YELLOW LEAVES: NOT A SIGN OF FALL

While yellow leaves are typically associated with the onset of the fall season, it's important to note that this isn't always the case. Seeing yellow leaves on your little herbling in the middle of a hot summer month can be quite disheartening!

**The cause:** For the most part, yellow leaves on herb plants are a sign of overwatering or even a lack of nutrients. Overwatering causes roots to become oxygen-starved, which results in the leaves and stems turning yellow. Additionally, a lack of nutrients can also cause leaves to turn yellow. In fact, both of these instances are causing your herblings to die.

**The solution:** In this instance, the solution depends on the actual cause. If you're not sure whether or not you may be overwatering your plant, be sure to follow my watering guidelines in Chapter 4. If, on the other hand, you suspect a lack of nutrients, opt for adding a balanced, organic fertilizer to help restore the nutrient levels. It may be necessary to do a pH soil test to determine which nutrient is lacking. Keep in mind, though, that some herbs require specific nutrients to boost growth.

## SLOW GROWTH: IT'S NOT YOU, IT'S THE HERBS

Often, when referring to a slow process, people sometimes refer to it as being like *watching paint dry.* Well, let me tell you, rushing out to your courtyard containers or backyard every morning hoping to see a little green sprout can feel like a slow, uneven process. This is especially accurate since a sign of something green is ultimately a sign of success.

**The cause**: Slow growth can be a result of three crucial factors—poor lighting, incorrect watering procedures, and even a too-high or too-low temperature.

**The solution:** If your herbs are taking longer than expected to sprout or seem to be stuck at a few inches, you will need to check all three factors to determine which one could be the culprit.

- **Lighting:** Keep in mind that most herbs require a considerable amount of light to grow the way they should. This usually means they'll need direct sun for between six to eight hours every day. Ensure that your windowsill and container pots are facing south. Rotate them where necessary or invest in grow lights as discussed in Chapter 4.
- **Watering:** As I've mentioned in the previous section, over and underwatering can cause yellow leaves and a lack of oxygen. Your little herb's growth will also be stunted, so, I recommend opting for the drip irrigation method or soaker hose as discussed in Chapter 4. Be sure to add additional leaves, twigs, and rocks to the bottom of your pots or containers to facilitate better drainage. You may also want to invest in a moisture meter to ensure that the soil is not too wet.
- **Temperature:** As I've mentioned in Chapter 11, growing your herbs in the right season is crucial

to their success. It's important to remember that most herbs prefer a temperature of between 60–70°F. To ensure that you're within the right temperature range, consider investing in a simple indoor thermometer such as the one you get from ThermoPro. Stick to the guidelines about the best times and conditions to plant your seeds or little herblings.

## WILTED PLANTS: MORE THAN JUST A SAD PLANT

Perhaps the only thing sadder than no little green shoots popping up out of the ground is watching a little plant start growing and then all of a sudden stop. Wilted herbs are a terribly depressing sight.

**The cause:** Generally, wilted plants are a sign of root rot, under-watering, and even a pest infestation. Fortunately, there are a few effective ways of dealing with all of these issues.

**The solution:** As with slow growth, you will need to review all three leading causes to ensure that you can best tackle the potential problem.

- **Root rot:** Overwatering is the number one cause of root rot, especially if excessive watering occurs continuously. It may also happen as a result of improper drainage. To remedy the situation, remove the affected plant and improve the drainage to prevent further issues. Use the tips already mentioned to ensure that you're not overwatering.

- **Underwatering:** In an attempt to avoid overwatering your herbs, you may actually end up underwatering them. It really is a fine line! The good news is that under-watered plants will quickly perk up if you increase the water. However, if the little herbling remains wilted after you have increased the water, it may be a sign that something else is wrong such as a possible disease or pest infestation.
- **Pest infestation:** Wilting is a common problem caused by aphids. Use my guidelines in Chapter 5 to identify pests. Fortunately, aphids can easily be removed using a mild soapy solution made up of dish soap and warm water, sprayed onto the offending leaves. Be sure to not drench the leaves.

## SPOTS ON LEAVES: AN UNWANTED GARDEN TREND

Herb leaves should be a healthy green color without spots or marks on them. If your weekly checks show spots on your leaves, it's important to get to the root of the problem before your whole plant is affected.

**The cause:** Spots on your herb leaves are usually a sign of fungal infection which develops on plants that are constantly wet. That means if you're overwatering, or your containers are under a leaking pipe or roof, your little herbs will be susceptible to bacteria and fungi growth.

**The solution:** To avoid fungus and bacteria growth on your plants, opt to water your plants from the base instead of from the top of the plant. Try to keep the leaves dry as much as possible. You should also treat the herb and the surrounding garden with an organic fungicide.

## LEGGY PLANTS: NOT AS GLAMOUROUS AS THEY SOUND

Essentially, a plant is referred to as *leggy* when it has grown very tall but features few leaves. It's important to not confuse a leggy plant with one that's growing well. A plant that seems to have had a sudden growth spurt but doesn't have a lot of leaves can be equally worrisome, especially since the leaves are what you'll want to harvest eventually.

**The cause:** In short, leggy herbs are a result of the little plant stretching toward the light. While you may think that a stretched-out, scraggly-looking plant can't be saved, the good news is that with the right treatment, it can easily become full again.

**The solution:** Since the only real cause of a plant becoming leggy has to do with it trying to reach for more light, the problem is usually quite easy to resolve. Consider moving pots and containers to a sunnier location. You may have to do the same with your backyard garden. To avoid creating additional work for yourself, be sure to follow the guidelines laid out in Chapter 4 about finding the most prominent light.

If you're not really sure whether your outdoor space gets the relevant light, you may want to place an herb in a pot in the exact space that you're considering. That way, you'll be able to see if an herbling will grow there before digging up the whole backyard! Furthermore, ensure that you're regularly pruning the area around the herb garden as other plants may literally be stealing your herb's light, causing your little plant to try to stretch up for some light. For indoor plants, a grow light may be a viable alternative if rotating the plant doesn't seem to be changing your plant's legginess.

## INEFFECTIVE HARVESTING: A RISKY SNIP-SNIP

Harvesting your herbs correctly will take some practice. Not only will this affect the herb leaves or flowers that you've harvested for drying and storage, but it may also leave you with plants that seem unable to grow another season, despite being perennials.

**The cause:** Over or underharvesting can leave your herb damaged and reduce the potential for future growth.

**The solution:** To ensure that your herbs are harvested correctly, please follow the steps I shared in Chapter 6. Keep in mind that not all herbs are harvested in the same way or even at the same time. For the most part, herbs should be harvested in the morning when their oil concentrations are at their highest.

Doing this will ensure the longest shelf life as well as maintain the best flavor. Another crucial tip to keep in mind is making sure your scissors are sharp. Use a sharp pair of garden, pruning, or kitchen scissors to make clean cuts without risking damage to the stems and stalks.

## LACKLUSTER FLAVOR: MISSING THE HERB IN HERB GARDEN

The number one reason people grow herbs is for the flavor they add to a dish. That said, it can be extremely disappointing to grow and harvest your herb only to discover that it tastes bland or adds no real flavor to your food!

**The cause:** Herbs can lack flavor due to poor soil quality, incorrect harvesting, or the old culprit, overwatering. Luckily, these are all fixable with a little effort.

**The solution:** As I've already mentioned, if your herb is experiencing a problem that can have multiple causes, the best solution is to start at a point and work your way down the list of potential issues. To overcome lackluster flavor, check out these three factors:

- **Poor soil quality:** It's often difficult to tell healthy soil from nutrient-lacking versions by simply looking at it unless you can see outright that it's dry clay. If you're planting in a new area or using soil that you've never seen anything growing in, I always recommend doing a soil pH test. That will identify what type of nutrient is lacking to make the soil as healthy as possible. Always opt for organic compost and fertilizer to enrich your soil.
- **Incorrect harvesting:** As mentioned in the previous hurdle, the time and way in which you harvest matters a great deal. Always harvest your herbs when their concentration of oils is at its peak. This will ensure the best possible flavor profile. Be sure to opt for freezing herbs in oil rather than drying them to ensure maximum flavor.
- **Overwatering:** The easiest way to overcome overwatering is to create a drip irrigation system and stick to a consistent watering schedule. Refer to all the previous guidelines to combat overwatering which in turn eliminates a bunch of problems, including a diluted flavor.

Many things can go wrong with your herb garden. Fortunately, for every problem, there's a tried and tested solution that will get your herb garden on track. If you're planting more than one type of herb, or you're starting off with a larger garden right off the bat, it's a good idea to keep an herb journal. Record problems and obstacles as well as what you did to overcome these issues. Be sure to highlight the solutions that worked best. That way, you'll make the following season considerably easier and more effective! Above all else, don't give up when you encounter a few problems in your new herb garden—adjust your strategy, use my guide to help you troubleshoot your challenge, and keep going!

**Spread the Seeds of Knowledge!**

There are few things more satisfying than harvesting your own herbs whenever the fancy strikes you... and this is your chance to pass that possibility on to more new gardeners.

Simply by sharing your honest opinion of this book and a little about your own gardening experience, you'll help other beginners find all the guidance they need to reap the abundant rewards of a thriving herb garden.

# LEAVE A REVIEW!

Thank you so much for your support. Happy gardening!
**Scan the QR code below to leave your review!**

# CONCLUSION

*Herbs should be used first as medicine, and then as seasoning.*

— OLD IRISH SAYING

One of the top inspirations for writing this guide came to me from listening to numerous people complimenting me on my garden and then follow it up with "It must have been difficult to get started" or "It must be expensive and time-consuming to maintain." I wanted to create a guide that proves it's neither expensive nor overly complex to create the herb garden of your dreams —especially when there are so many reasons why everyone should be able to have even the smallest herb garden!

For instance, there are the multitudes of health benefits that go along with adding fresh, organic herbs to your food. And don't even get me started on the taste—believe me, it's true that once you grow and taste your own herbs, you'll never go back to store-bought again! After all, if you can grow your own herbs, why would you return to eating expensive, pesticide-filled herbs that have little to no nutritional value by the time they get to you?

With this guide, I've strived to give you a little more insight into the simplicity of herb gardening. My aim, when I started, was to show you that you don't need expensive equipment, acres of land, and a small fortune to get started. All you really need is a pot, soil, an herb, decent sunlight, water, and—of course—your enthusiasm!

If you're half as enthusiastic and determined as I have been to make my herb garden work, then you'll use the tips I've shared combined with your resources and before you know it, you'll have a garden—even if it's just a few small windowsill pots.

Another huge advantage is that you don't need to research and download complicated recipes from the internet to use your fresh herbs. Simply cook the food you currently enjoy but replace the dried store-bought herbs with a few sprigs from your garden. Never be afraid to experiment with your current recipes by removing certain herbs and replacing them with new and exciting flavors.

Set organic methods for sustainable herb gardening that I have shared. When searching for containers, adopt the mantra of *reuse, recycle, or repurpose*. Stick to organic fertilizer, mulch, compost, and pest control methods. Never forget that you are going to serve those herbs in food for your loved ones, which means your number one goal should always be to grow them as organically as possible!

My list of potential gardening hurdles you may encounter should make it easy for you to spot a challenge in its infancy and save your herb before it wilts or infects the rest of your plants. On that note, watch the watering techniques.

Yes, friends, it really is that simple! With this, I urge you to start that herb garden you've always dreamed of. If you're feeling hesitant, start small—plant a pot of parsley and rosemary on your kitchen windowsill. And when they're still alive after two weeks, spoil yourself with another two herbs. Opt for cuttings from existing healthy plants to give your confidence a boost. Keep adding a small pot of a different herb until your windowsill is full!

In closing, I want to reiterate my sentiment that herb gardening is easy enough for anyone to do, with the resources they have available. This guide is proof that it doesn't have to be complicated either. I hope that you will find as much joy and satisfaction in your herb gardening adventure as I have in mine. Thank you for embarking on this wonderful herb gardening journey with me!

*Happy herbing!*

*If you've enjoyed reading this guide as much as I have loved creating it, then it would be great it you would please leave a positive review. More positive reviews make it easier for other budding herb gardeners to find this guide and take advantage of the tips and suggestions shared.*

# BONUS SECTION

---

*If you've never experienced the joy of accomplishing more than you can imagine, plant a garden.*

— ROBERT BRAULT

---

Reading this easy-to-follow guide is one thing. Remembering everything when you're ankle-deep in soil and mulch is perhaps another story altogether! With that in mind, I've decided to spare you the stress of flipping back to those watering tips I shared by compiling a list of the most useful herb gardening tips in one easy-to-find section. Yes, that's how much I want you to embrace your herb gardening journey! Find the 99 most significant tips below.

## 99 USEFUL HERB GARDEN TIPS IN ONE EASY-TO-FIND SECTION

### *It's Easy*

[1] Herbs are easy to grow, no matter how big or small your space is.

[2] Containers, pots, vertical arrangements, and outdoor backyards are all excellent locations for an herb garden.

[3] Reuse old containers for planting, it's a fun and eco-friendly way to garden.

[4] If you only have limited space, opt for the top three, or five herbs that you're going to use for cooking, teas, or medicine.

[5] Consider hanging a few plant baskets or even a vertical garden to provide more space.

[6] Grow parsley indoors, it's easy and you can have fresh herbs even in winter.

[7] Dill is another herb that's simple to grow and can thrive both indoors and outdoors.

[8] Thyme is a hardy herb that requires little care, making it a sustainable choice for any gardener.

[9] Mint is fast-growing and can easily spread, providing you with a plentiful supply.

[10] Sage is a hardy herb that can tolerate cold winters.

[11] Oregano is a perennial herb; it'll keep coming back every year.

[12] Marjoram is great for container gardening; it doesn't need a lot of space.

[13] Basil is a sun-lover, perfect for a sunny windowsill or a spot in your backyard.

[14] Chives are super easy to grow, and they come back year after year.

[15] Cilantro loves cool weather, plant it in the spring or fall for the best results.

[16] Indoor herb gardens can provide fresh herbs year-round while saving water and space.

### Light Above All Else

[17] The most important consideration when setting up your herb garden is a location with the right amount of light.

[18] That can be anything between four to six hours, depending on your area and the herb you've selected. To be on the safe side, always opt for at least six hours.

[19] Create your outdoor garden in rows so that you have space for row covers in the winter.

### Understand Growth Characteristics

[20] As tempted as you might be to buy seed packs and little herblings of all sorts, it's important to understand the growth characteristics of the top five you've shortlisted.

[21] Mint is a good example of understanding growth characteristics. Few beginners know that these wonderful herbs spread underground and sprout shoots all over the garden. Always keep your mint in a container to avoid it from overwhelming the other herbs.

### Difference Between Annuals and Perennials

[22] Always check whether any new additions are annuals or perennials. This is important if you want to have herbs in your garden all year round.

[23] Knowing whether you have annuals or perennials determines the amount of seasonal care you need to invest in your garden. You can then plan the best ways to care for your herbs during the colder months when you don't really want to be in the garden.

### The Right Soil

[24] Loamier soil is always a great option for outdoor gardens, while a high-quality potting soil mix is the perfect option for indoor pots and containers.

[25] If you've never grown anything in the area you're considering, and you've never seen anything other than

weeds grow there, you may have to perform a simple pH test on the soil so that you can determine its nutritional requirements.

[26] Enhance your soil by digging deeply and adding organic matter, it gives plants a good start.

[27] Herbs aren't too picky, but well-draining soil is a must. Mix in some compost to improve the soil's texture. Different herbs prefer slightly different soil types, so tailor it to your plants. For instance, rosemary likes it a bit sandy, while basil prefers rich, loamy soil.

### Correct Drainage

[28] Always choose a gardening setup with drainage in mind. Containers and pots should have drainage holes and pot trays or saucers.

[29] You can improve drainage by adding a mix of leaves, twigs, and rocks to the bottom of your pot or container.

[30] To improve drainage in your backyard space, dig a few small trenches that run along next to your herb rows —this will drain excess water away and prevent it from pooling on your herbs.

### Plant Companions

[31] If you're planting in large pots, or in a backyard space, consider planting companion plants as these will support your herbs by using their fragrance to chase away

unwanted pests or provide shade from an overbearing sun.

[32] Simple veggies such as tomatoes and carrots are great companions for just about all herbs and they add to your ingredients to use in the garden.

[33] However, if you only want an herb garden, opt for variations that complement each other.

### The Right Tools

[34] Invest in the right tools for your garden work. Sharp, clean tools will not only make the process so much easier but will also keep your herbs safe.

[35] Be sure to sterilize your garden tools regularly to avoid diseases spreading between plants. This is especially necessary when you're growing herbs in one area and regular flowers and shrubs in another, as cross-contamination can easily occur.

### The Instructions

[36] Always follow the instructions on seed packets or those that come with the seedlings.

[37] If you're getting a cutting from a fellow gardener, place it in a rooting hormone to get the growth process started.

[38] Join local community groups or even US-based social media groups. You will learn valuable tips that apply to your specific climate and growing conditions.

## *Watering*

[39] Practice your watering technique from day one to ensure that you don't over or underwater.

[40] Water your little herbs early in the morning to avoid losing the water to evaporation.

[41] Don't water over the leaves, but rather around it, or in the tray for the soil to suck up.

[42] Avoid overwatering as it starves the roots of oxygen. Your goal is to have moist, not drenched soil.

[43] Let the top inch of soil dry out before watering. The best way to check is to stick your finger in there. If it's dry, give them a drink. Be mindful of not soaking them; herbs like to keep their feet (roots) dry!

[44] Consider drip irrigation or soaker hose methods to make watering more efficient.

[45] Use a rain gauge to monitor how much water your outdoor garden is getting from rainfall.

### Heed the Signs

[46] Herbs should be a healthy green color with robust roots.

[47] Look out for brown stems, yellow leaves, soft roots, and heavy leaf fall as this is an indication of disease or overwatering.

[48] Be wary of long spaces between leaf nodes as this can be a sign that your herbling is not getting enough light.

[49] One of the joys of herbs is their delightful fragrance. Healthy herb plants will release a strong, pleasant scent when you gently rub or crush their leaves. If the aroma is weak or unpleasant, it might be a sign of an issue.

[50] When repotting or transplanting, take a peek at the roots. Healthy roots should be white or light tan and firm. If they appear brown, slimy, or have a foul odor, root rot may be present. Trim away affected roots and repot in fresh soil.

### Fertilizing

[51] If necessary, apply fertilizer in the early spring just as the roots are starting to grow.

[52] Follow the instructions on the fertilizer container or bag and never give more fertilizer than necessary.

[53] Always opt for organic fertilizer as you want the herbs to be as healthy and nutritious as possible—remember, you're going to eat them!

[54] Compost kitchen scraps to create nutrient-rich soil for your herbs.

[55] Use coffee grounds as fertilizer, they're rich in nitrogen which herbs love.

### Keep an Eye Out for Pests

[56] Insects such as aphids, snails, slugs, and weevils all love the taste of your herbs as much as you do.

[57] Check your herbs regularly for signs of leave damage, wilting, and furry residue on the leaves.

[58] Use organic methods to rid the infected plant and wherever possible, avoid harmful pesticide chemicals as these are toxic and may make the herb unusable.

[59] Plant bee-friendly herbs like lavender and borage, they attract pollinators.

[60] Use eggshells as natural pest deterrent, they'll keep snails and slugs at bay.

### Harvesting

[61] Most herbs should be harvested just before they flower as the flavor profile of the herb is the strongest at that point.

[62] Use clean tools to gently cut the leaves during harvesting.

[63] Harvest your herbs in the morning, just after the dew has dried. This is when their essential oils are the most concentrated.

[64] Avoid harvesting more than a third of the plant at once. You want to leave enough leaves for the plant to continue growing.

[65] Don't forget about our pollinator friends! Leave a few flowers or branches on your herbs for bees and other beneficial insects.

[66] Choose the best leaves for harvesting - the ones that are young, healthy, and free from any blemishes or discoloration.

### *Storing*

[67] After harvesting, rinse and dry your herbs properly before storage.

[68] Dry your herbs in a cool, dark area such as your pantry, or chop them up and store them in an ice cube tray infused with olive oil.

[69] Herbs not frozen for storage should always be stored in a cool, dark place in an airtight container.

[70] Make your own herb-infused oils. Fill a clean, dry jar with herbs, cover with oil (like olive or sunflower oil), and

let it sit for a couple of weeks. Strain, and you'll have a flavorful oil for cooking.

[71] Another delicious option is herb butter. Mix chopped herbs with softened butter, roll it into a log, wrap in plastic or wax paper, and freeze. Slice off portions as needed.

### Cooking

[72] Adding herbs to your cooking process early on may cause the flavor to draw out too much.

[73] For a richer flavor burst, always add softer herbs to the dish just before serving.

[74] Don't be afraid to experiment with different herbs and make note of your favorite pairings so that you can repeat them!

[75] Whenever possible, use fresh herbs. They have more flavor than dried ones.

[76] To release the full aroma and flavor of herbs, chop them finely just before adding to your dish. A sharp knife works wonders!

[77] Herbs can be powerful, so taste your dish as you go. You can always add more if needed, but it's hard to fix an overly herb-y dish.

### *Health Benefits*

[78] Herbs have a multitude of health benefits and if your goal is to make healthier food choices, opt for herbs that have the most nutritional value.

[79] You can add them to cooked meals, salads, smoothies, desserts, and even ice cream.

[80] Using herbs allows you to cut back on salt. They add flavor without the need for excessive sodium, which is great for maintaining healthy blood pressure.

[81] Certain herbs like mint and ginger can help soothe your stomach and ease digestion. You can make herbal teas or add them to your dishes for a tummy-friendly touch.

[82] Many herbs, such as garlic, thyme, and oregano, have immune-boosting properties. They can help your body fend off illnesses.

[83] Aromatherapy using herbs like lavender and chamomile can promote relaxation and reduce stress. A cup of herbal tea before bedtime can work wonders.

[84] Gardening and using herbs in your cooking can be therapeutic. It's a fantastic way to relieve stress and stimulate your creativity.

### *Opt for Propagation*

[85] It's a good idea to start your herbs from propagation. Using cuttings from healthy parent plants is an excellent way to ensure that the herbs you're going to harvest will be of the same quality as the parent plant.

[86] Always use healthy stems for cuttings and use a root hormone to boost growth. You can also dip the stem in honey, which is a natural root hormone.

[87] Be sure to acclimatize your little herb before planting it in your backyard. This process takes place between seven to ten days after the first roots appear.

### *Choose Variety*

[88] While most people only know the names of a few herbs off hand, it's important to keep in mind that there are thousands of options to choose from.

[89] The more diverse your herb garden is, the more cooking and medicinal benefits you can enjoy.

[90] Don't be afraid to choose a few unusual herbs, especially the perennials that will ensure you have flavorful herbs to use even in the winter months.

[91] When opting for unusual herbs, always read up on their growth requirements, soil type, as well as water and light requirements.

### Climate Care

[92] Ensure that you water your herbs adequately in the spring and summer months to avoid them drying out.

[93] Annuals should be completely harvested at the beginning of autumn as they will start wilting at the first sign of frost.

[94] Winter care can involve adding extra mulch, additional insulation on pots and containers, as well as putting up row covers.

[95] For areas that experience extreme rain, consider lifting the container pots to avoid them becoming drenched.

[96] You may need to dig drainage holes in your backyard garden to get excess water flowing away from your herbs.

### Troubleshooting Your Challenges

[97] There will be challenges. Some herbs, despite your best efforts, will not reach harvesting. It doesn't make you a bad gardener—these things happen!

[98] Avoid the more significant gardening hurdles by using cuttings or little plants that have passed the seed stage, if you like.

[99] Look out for yellowing leaves ahead of fall as this is always a sign that somewhere, something is wrong.

[100] Check that leggy or wilted plants have the right amount of sunlight and also be wary of pests and potential plant disease. Since over or underwatering is often a common reason for many herb-growing problems, this is the best place to start looking for causes of potential problems.

## UNDERSTANDING YOUR ZONE HARDINESS

To be successful at planting your herb garden, it helps to have a clear understanding of the USDA Plant Hardiness Zone Map (United States Department of Agriculture, 2020) Essentially, this is the standard that growers and gardeners use to determine which plant types are most likely to thrive in a specific location. This map is drawn up using the average annual minimum winter temperature, which is then divided into 10-degree F zones and further divided into 5-degree F half-zones.

To see if the herbs you want to grow are compatible with your specific geographical area, simply visit the USDA Plant Hardiness Zone Map website at planthardiness.ars.usda.gov.

Once you have checked out the zone hardiness for your area, all that's left is for you to decide where you want to plant your beautiful herb garden and get started. Remember, it's easier than you think!

**Happy planting and enjoy your herbs!**

# REFERENCES

Avisomo Modular Farming. (2021, October 28). *Why are LED grow lights best for vertical farming?* Avisomo. https://avisomo.com/why-is-led-best-for-efficient-plant-growth/#:

Besemer, T. (2021, May 10). *15 herbs to propagate from cuttings & how to do it.* Rural Sprout. https://www.ruralsprout.com/propagate-herbs-from-cuttings/

Biggs, C. (2021, April 13). *How to propagate your favorite herbs, such as rosemary, mint, basil, and more.* Martha Stewart. https://www.marthastewart.com/8090164/how-propagate-herbs

Cariaga, V. (2023, April 13). *The average American is spending $253 A month more on groceries, gas, and other items compared to last year.* Yahoo Finance. https://finance.yahoo.com/news/average-american-spending-253-month-171430612.html

Coviello, N. (2022, May 31). *7 Reasons to grow an indoor herb garden.* Vegan ShowOff. https://veganshowoff.com/reasons-to-grow-an-indoor-herb-garden/

Deering, S. (2019, February 28). *Nature's 9 most powerful medicinal plants and the science behind them.* Healthline; Healthline Media. https://www.healthline.com/health/most-powerful-medicinal-plants

Denby, L. (2018, June 5). *The ultimate guide to cooking with fresh herbs.* Taste of Home. https://www.tasteofhome.com/article/the-ultimate-guide-to-cooking-with-fresh-herbs/

Doyle, S. (2021, May 19). *16 Herb gardening mistakes you don't want to make.* Gardening. https://gardening.org/16-herb-gardening-mistakes-you-dont-want-to-make/

Ewumi, O. (2022, October 6). *Herbal medicine: Types, uses, and safety.* Www.medicalnewstoday.com. https://www.medicalnewstoday.com/articles/herbal-medicine

Exarchou, V., Nenadis, N., Tsimidou, M., Gerothanassis, I. P., Troganis, A., & Boskou, D. (2002). Antioxidant activities and phenolic composition of extracts from Greek oregano, Greek sage, and summer savory. *Journal of Agricultural and Food Chemistry, 50*(19), 5294–5299. https://doi.org/10.1021/jf020408a

Filipic, M. (2015, May 13). *Horticulture educator offers top 10 tips for planting herbs.* Cfaes.osu.edu. https://cfaes.osu.edu/news/articles/horticulture-educator-offers-top-10-tips-for-planting-herbs

Grange, R. I., & Loach, K. (1985). The effect of light on the rooting of leafy cuttings. *Scientia Horticulturae, 27*(1-2), 105–111. https://doi.org/10.1016/0304-4238(85)90060-3

H, J. (2022, February 12). *What type of fertilizer is best for your herbs?* The culinary herb garden. https://howtoculinaryherbgarden.com/fertilizer-for-herbs/

JamieOliver.com. (2016, May 11). *How to cook with herbs | Features.* Jamie Oliver. https://www.jamieoliver.com/features/how-to-use-herbs/

Karadsheh, S. (2022, April 21). *Best way to store fresh herbs (2 Easy Methods).* The Mediterranean Dish. https://www.themediterraneandish.com/how-to-store-fresh-herbs/

Kim. (2023, July 29). *Organic methods for pest control in the garden.* Shiplap and Shells. https://shiplapandshells.com/natural-and-organic-garden-pest-control/

Kring, L. (2022, September 4). *How to winterize your herb garden | Gardener's Path.* Gardener's Path. https://gardenerspath.com/plants/herbs/winterize-herb-garden/

Kring, L. (2023, April 7). *Spring care tips for your herb garden.* Gardener's Path. https://gardenerspath.com/plants/herbs/spring-care-tips/#:

Lofgren, K. (2015, January 3). *How to create a vertical garden.* Gardener's Path. https://gardenerspath.com/how-to/design/vertical-gardening-works-everyone/

Lofgren, K. (2023, April 12). *How to grow and use lovage, An uncommon herb.* Gardener's Path. https://www.gardenerspath.com/plants/vegetables/growing-lovage-uncommon-leafy-green-many-uses/

MacArthur, A. (2023, September 5). *The best mulch for an herb garden you can make or buy.* Food Gardening Network. https://foodgardening.mequoda.com/daily/spice-herb-gardening/the-best-mulch-for-an-herb-garden-you-can-make-or-buy/

Parlin, J., Filer, P., Mcdonald, D., Stork, J., & Parker, J. (2021). *Growing herbs for the health of it!* https://extension.arizona.edu/sites/extension. arizona.edu/files/pubs/az1922-2021.pdf

Pino, M. (2023, July 9). *10 Benefits of vertical gardening.* Planet Natural. https://www.planetnatural.com/10-benefits-of-vertical-gardening/

Rahbardar, M., & Hosseinzadeh, H. (2020). Therapeutic effects of rosemary (Rosmarinus officinalis L.) and its active constituents on nervous system disorders. *Therapeutic Effects of Rosemary (Rosmarinus Officinalis L.) and Its Active Constituents on Nervous System Disorders, 23*(9). https://doi.org/10.22038/ijbms.2020.45269.10541

Rose, S. (2023, February 17). *How often to water herbs—Avoid overwatering.* Garden Therapy. https://gardentherapy.ca/how-often-to-water-herbs/

Sherry, D. (2014, April 25). *Coping With powdery mildew.* FineGardening. https://www.finegardening.com/project-guides/gardening-basics/coping-with-powdery-mildew

Shiffler, A. (2020, June 16). *15 rare herbs you should consider growing in your garden.* Herbs at Home. https://herbsathome.co/15-rare-herbs-to-grow-in-your-garden/

Sung, E. (2018, July 12). *13 Fresh herbs and how to use them.* Epicurious; Epicurious. https://www.epicurious.com/ingredients/fresh-herbs-how-to-use-them-article

Svedi, R. (2021, July 23). *Propagating herbs in the garden.* Gardening Know How. https://www.gardeningknowhow.com/edible/herbs/hgen/propagation-in-your-herb-garden.htm

thearchspace, & ARCHSPACE, T. (2022, September 13). *Vertical Gardening – brief, pros, and cons · the archspace.* The Archspace. https://thearchspace.com/vertical-gardening-brief-pros-and-cons/

United States Department of Agriculture. (2020). *USDA Plant Hardiness Zone Map.* Usda.gov. https://planthardiness.ars.usda.gov/

University of Rochester Medical Center. (2014). *A guide to common medicinal herbs - health encyclopedia - University of Rochester Medical Center.* Rochester.edu. https://www.urmc.rochester.edu/encyclopedia/content.aspx?contenttypeid=1&contentid=1169

VanDerZanden, A. M. (2008, January). *Environmental factors affecting plant growth.* OSU Extension Service; Oregon State University. https://

extension.oregonstate.edu/gardening/techniques/environmental-factors-affecting-plant-growth

Walsh, S. (2004, May 12). *Plant propagation.* Ucanr.edu. https://ucanr.edu/sites/mgslo/newsletters/plant_propagation28245.htm

World Health Organisation. (2010, May 6). *A healthy lifestyle - WHO recommendations.* World Health Organisation. https://www.who.int/europe/news-room/fact-sheets/item/a-healthy-lifestyle---who-recommendations

Yoon, A., Oh, H. E., Kim, S. Y., & Park, Y. G. (2021). Plant growth regulators and rooting substrates affect the growth and development of Salix koriyanagi cuttings. *Rhizosphere, 20*(100437), 100437. https://doi.org/10.1016/j.rhisph.2021.100437

Made in the USA
Las Vegas, NV
12 December 2024

13933443R00108